BROADMOOR

MY JOURNEY INTO HELL

BROADMOOR

MY JOURNEY INTO HELL

CHARLIE BRONSON

WITH LORRAINE ETHERINGTON

JOHN BLAKE

Published by
John Blake Publishing Limited
3 Bramber Court, 2 Bramber Road
London W14 9PB

www.johnblakepublishing.co.uk

www.facebook.com/johnblakebooks 🖪
twitter.com/jblakebooks 🗉

First published in hardback in 2015

ISBN: 978-1-78418-117-8

British Library Cataloguing-in-Publication Data:

A catalogue record for this book is available from the British Library.

Design by www.envydesign.co.uk

Printed in Great Britain by CPI Group (UK) Ltd

1 3 5 7 9 10 8 6 4 2

Papers used by John Blake Publishing are natural, recyclable products made
from wood grown in sustainable forests. The manufacturing processes
conform to the environmental regulations of the country of origin.

Every attempt has been made to contact the relevant copyright-holders,
but some were unobtainable. We would be grateful if the appropriate
people could contact us.

TO ALL RMOs

I have got a request to accept a patient from Rampton,
a man called Peterson, a schizophrenic and dangerous.
I've said I'll only take him on a swap basis.

Have you got anyone ?

PG McG

7 August 1979

Not me

Internal memo to all staff. *'Swapsies? What is this, a fucking card game? This
is my life they're playing with!'* – Charlie Bronson

CONTENTS

FOREWORD — IX

INTRODUCTION — XV

BROADMOOR: A BRIEF HISTORY — 1

PART 1 BROADMOOR CRIMINAL LUNATIC ASYLUM, 1979–84

CHAPTER 1: WELCOME TO THE LUNATIC ASYLUM — 11

CHAPTER 2: GLOUCESTER HOUSE — 35

CHAPTER 3: NORFOLK INTENSIVE CARE UNIT — 51

CHAPTER 4: KENT BLOCK (WARD 3) — 67

CHAPTER 5: NORFOLK BLOCK — 81

CHAPTER 6: UP ON THE ROOF PART I (21 MAY 1981) — 87

CHAPTER 7: UP ON THE ROOF PART II, DAY 1 (19 JUNE 1983) — 103

CHAPTER 8: UP ON THE ROOF PART II, DAY 2   111
    (20 JUNE 1983)

CHAPTER 9: UP ON THE ROOF PART II, DAYS 3 AND 4   115
    (21–2 JUNE 1983)

CHAPTER 10: ROOF III: MY HAT TRICK (GIVE ME THE   131
    FUCKING BALL!) (14 MARCH 1984)

CHAPTER 11: SECLUSION   139

CHAPTER 12: REFLECTIONS OF MY MIND   147

PART 2 OTHER MADNESS

CHAPTER 13: THE MANURE HEAP AND   153
    OTHER MADNESS

CHAPTER 14: BROADMITES BOUND   173

EPILOGUE   179
POSTSCRIPT – OCTOBER 2014   183
APPENDIX I BROADMOOR: FAMOUS INMATES   185
APPENDIX II DRUGS INDEX   195
APPENDIX III OFFICIAL CHANGE OF NAME   199
BIBLIOGRAPHY   203

FOREWORD

LORRAINE ETHERINGTON

I first heard about Charlie Bronson when I stumbled on a website supporting his release. As I learned more of the facts of his case and his history, I felt a burning and overwhelming sense of injustice. I proceeded to spend a large part of my time writing letters to various government ministerial departments to complain about Charlie's continued imprisonment, which I believed to be totally unnecessary. How could the British government justify caging a man for over four decades, a man who'd never killed? I also couldn't understand why he was serving life for false imprisonment, or why he had to be kept behind a double-doored cage in what was dubbed 'Monster Mansion', a place supposedly designed to hold murderers and sexual offenders. Charlie was neither. How utterly futile and inhumane it was. Was he really as dangerous as the media had spent years convincing us he was?

It didn't occur to me until some months later that I could write to the man himself. But what does one say? What can be written that hasn't been written a hundred times before? I confined my correspondence to light reading of a cheerful nature, in the hope that it would briefly take him outside of the cell he occupied for twenty-three hours a day. After some months he wrote to say that he would like to add me to his telephone list. If I were to write this foreword without divulging the following it would, quite simply, be a travesty. Our first call went something like this:

Charles Bronson: *'Allo? Is that Lorraine?*

Lorraine: *Yes.*

CB: *This is Charlie.*

This man didn't sound anything like the Charlie Bronson I had come to imagine. I don't know what I imagined exactly, perhaps the growling, low baritone voice that would accompany a massive bearded creature that lived in a cage. The voice on the end of the phone was cheery, light and happy – he sounded just like a little cockney sparra singing in my ear. I decided that this wasn't Charlie Bronson.

LE: *Who?*

CB: *It's Charrrrleeee.*

I figured someone was winding me up and my brain ticked over furiously, trying to think who it could be. You'd have to get up earlier than this to catch me out.

LE: *No you're not.*

CB: *What?*

LE: *Who is this?*

CB: *It's Char-lee!*

I then ploughed on for a good minute or two, accusing him of being several people I suspected were behind this ruse, while his precious phone units flew by in front of his eyes. He seemed quite sure he was Charlie, so I thought I'd play along with it.

LE: *OK, yes, alright, you're Charlie Bronson. Course you are. Crack on then mate.*

CB: *What?*

LE: *Go on, carry on.*

CB: *Well, what do you want me to say? I AM Charlie.*

LE: *Course you are sunshine.*

CB: *Fucking hell, I'm getting fed up of this. Listen... I got your postcards.*

I can honestly say it was one of those moments in life when a crater opening beneath you would be a welcome event. Luckily for me, Charlie's patience held. Meeting him would come as a natural progression from our letters and calls and this happened in December 2010, at the Close Supervision Centre of Wakefield Prison, Yorkshire.

Travel chaos abounded as heavy snow fell across the UK, threatening to cancel our first visit, but I made it. As the Yorkshire sleet fell and icy winds whipped at my face, I was escorted over to the unit by a lovely prison officer called Mr Chapman, a real old-school gentleman. By the time we reached the unit, I had to pay a visit to the little girls' room. The cold had gotten the better of my bladder.

Sat on the throne, I could hear this cockney voice shouting out, 'Oi, come on Lorraine, where are ya? What's going on? Come on. Oi?' My God, that's him shouting. What was I expecting when I walked into that small room divided in two by a wall with a small opening in it, just a set of bars through which we would have to converse? I knew it would certainly not be the bearded monster the newspapers were so keen to portray. But similarly, I didn't expect to be faced with such a bubbly, alert and cheery man. 'Hello!' he chirped. His famous handlebar moustache bristled, almost in defiance and we shook hands through the bars. 'THAT is an epic 'tache!' I said.

As we settled down and chatted, I felt a strange sense that I had known this man before. I felt instantly at ease and found him to be very engaging and warm. But there was one thing I was determined to ask: 'Would you take your glasses off please?' Whatever my fears about this man's sanity, I knew I would find the answer if I could just see his eyes. Someone once said that the eyes are the windows to the soul and I believe strongly that you can tell a lot about a person by their eyes. Be they vacant and empty or alert and wild, it is a good indicator to a person's state of mind. Charlie removed the iconic dark round specs that hid his eyes and I knew at that moment that this man was definitely of sane mind. His eyes were deep and questioning, and had an intensity to them that I was to witness many times over the course of time. My overriding feeling was that here was a man who possessed remarkable mental strength and courage, to survive everything he had, to endure the years of systematic abuse and the special hospitals. More remarkably, he had no bitterness about his experiences. I sensed a vulnerability that one simply would not associate with 'Britain's most violent prisoner'. He was candidly honest and had a genuine interest in people, an appetite to learn. When he spoke about himself, he was self-effacing and yet animated and vibrant. Above all, he was caring – and even a fool could see he was in need of some in return. He just wasn't Charles Bronson to me. He was Michael Peterson.

Some four years on, in helping to compile this book, I am left truly humbled on an almost daily basis by the man. Like many, I have read previous books and may have felt I knew a great deal about him. Having read through his account of his time in Broadmoor, I was left shocked, distressed and with a profound sense of anger for what he has endured. Only now has Charlie really divulged what happened at Broadmoor in his five-year tenure there. Before my involvement with this book, I would say I respected him for his indomitable spirit and his sense of humour. Having completed this remarkable account, I am privileged and honoured to be a small part of it. I can also say with complete candour that I can understand why, to some people, Charlie Bronson is an inspiration, an anti-hero. Perhaps after reading this, you will feel the same way. However, this is not about glorifying crime or a notorious criminal. This is about the journey of one man, Michael Peterson, and how he survived in impossible conditions. And once it is revealed to you exactly what those conditions were, perhaps, like me, you will agree, that this man is one remarkable human being. That he can still find it in his heart to have love, warmth and hope is a miracle. The injustice he suffered endures to this day with his continued imprisonment and total absence of rehabilitation. But like Mr Peterson, some of us have equal levels of determination and endurance, and will fight on, until justice is served. It is time to free Michael Peterson (aka Charlie Bronson).

P.S. Micky P, I love you.

LORRAINE ETHERINGTON

INTRODUCTION

If someone asked you to name the most famous prison on the planet, I guess it would be one of these: Alcatraz, Colditz, or San Quentin perhaps. But if it was the most feared asylum in our universe, it could be only one name: Broadmoor Criminal Lunatic Asylum. Let's cut the political correctness bollocks and face reality, Broadmoor is a creepy fucking place, it even sounds naughty (and believe me, it's even naughtier than it sounds). It is the closest place on earth that you will get to hell. It should have been called Hellmoor. Behind those walls is a very, very cold, cruel establishment and boy, do I know about it.

It was almost thirty-five years ago now that those gates opened up and sucked me in so deep that it crushed my soul. Nobody is ever the same again after living in that place. You don't just remember it: you smell it. That insane smell never leaves you. Those crazy screams stay in your head. The horror comes back over and over again in your nightmares. A Broadmoor inmate is forever branded. You can never escape it. You're an official Broadmite. You were born mad. Did you know that the first loons to arrive in Broadmoor got here on a cart-horse? A fucking cart-horse! Can you picture that? Fuck me, if that was me I'd have jumped off and made a run for it, or wrapped them up and rode off on horseback. John Wayne. Yeee-haaaaRRRR! Cor, it's changed a bit since then, eh? My moves are like SAS operations. I've about as much chance of escaping as a budgie superglued to a perch! That's what you get for being high profile sadly. I'm treated like some desperado. Public Enemy Number 1.

Well I think it's time for me to open up my brain and expose what really does happen in that God-forsaken sewer. It's been painful for me to relive what you are about to read, but I want to ensure it becomes public knowledge. So many stories of abuse and neglect are now coming out about Broadmoor. We're in a public age where much more is understood about mental illness. Back in my time in Broadmoor, a loon was a loon, we had no voice. Anything we said was obviously all in our mad minds. But today it's become evident what horrors hid behind the walls of Broadmoor, for years, decades and, yes, even over a century. Well, I want my time in that hellhole to go on record, for my family, and to hopefully help prevent others suffering the same as I did.

Don't worry though reader: it's not all gloom and doom. It's not been a bad life's journey for me, not when you can wake up with a sing-song and a smile. Despite all the naughtiness and insanity, it really is a wonderful world. That's quite something coming from a man who's mostly described as 'Britain's maddest, baddest and most violent prisoner'! What they fail to mention is that I am a loving, generous and affectionate man. I am, like everyone else, a human being. Broadmoor couldn't take that away from me, and it never broke me. I broke Broadmoor... and this is the story of how I did it.

I want to dedicate this story to Michael Martin.

Michael Martin was just twenty-two when he was sectioned under the Mental Health Act (1959) and sent to Broadmoor. On 6 July 1984 Michael was involved in a violent struggle with six guards (or 'nurses', as they called themselves) and he sustained physical injuries. He was taken into seclusion, restrained, stripped naked and injected with a heavy dosage of sedative by a 'nurse'. He had already been given a sedative earlier in the day and had also eaten a meal. It is believed that the cocktail of drugs administered led to him vomiting. Michael choked to death on his own sick. The subsequent post mortem revealed that Michael's body was 'imprinted with signs of lack of care indicative of, if not murder, then manslaughter. [sic] bruising around his neck was consistent with a neck hold which might have prevented the vomit from escaping in the usual way.'

The Ritchie Report (1985) into Michael's death found that the use of a neck hold was dangerous and should not have happened. This had caused deep and extensive bruising and may have contributed to Michael's vomiting and aspiration. A doctor was not in attendance and the wing Michael was on was shown to lack facilities. (E. Goldstein, 2004).

The Ritchie Report made five recommendations for change. It rejected the use of neck holds as a method of restraint and recommended that nursing staff should receive compulsory, regular training in control and restraint techniques, and that the minimum force required be used to control violence. In October 1984 a coroners' court returned a verdict of accidental death aggravated by a lack of care. Michael Martin was the first of three black patients to die in Broadmoor in conditions of control and restraint. Circa 1988/89 Joseph Watts was put into seclusion and injected with a cocktail of drugs following an incident with another patient. He died within minutes. In 1991 Orville Blackwood died in similar circumstances.

Michael is never forgotten by me. It was a very cruel ending for a smashing young fella. Michael arrived at Broadmoor only weeks after myself in 1979. He was just twenty-two years old when he came in, a real live wire and a good soul. He laughed a lot and was a lot of fun to be with. He was a black lad and proud of it. He was also fearless and had a way about him that I respected. He actually livened the place up. Most inmates were depressed and sluggish, drugged up, slow and clumsy. The authorities can try and call them 'patients' but they are prisoners. What else do you call it when the people inside are locked up? The staff try to call themselves 'nurses', yet they are members of the Prison Officers' Association. Nurses my arse!

The people inside Broadmoor are sick guys. Psychotics, schizoids, psychos, you name it, they are there. Mass murderers, poisoners, arsonists, cannibals, serial killers, sex offenders, and all other manner of horrible cunts. You can smell the evil dripping out of their pores. Some were very heavily sedated and they just slept day and night. Some would go for a shit and fall asleep on the toilet. Well, they soon had Michael on a similar cocktail of drugs. When he arrived he was about ten, maybe eleven stone, very fit and strong. He moved with great agility, like an athlete; he was always smiling and his eyes sparkled. When he spoke, he always had something worthwhile to say, intelligent. Over the course of the next four years I watched Broadmoor destroy him with psychotropic drugs. He put on about five stone, slept a lot and became very drawn and depressed. He became slow and he rarely smiled anymore. Suddenly he looked old. Fuck me, he was only a young lad. This was nothing but drug control and an abuse of power. It was heartbreaking to witness.

I met Michael's mother and sister several times on visits as Michael ended up on the infamous Norfolk Block with me. We were mostly kept in isolation in Norfolk but on visits we used to share a small room, so Michael got to meet some of my friends and family. His mother was a lovely lady with a beautiful smile. That smile was erased from her face on 6 July 1984. Michael didn't die; he was killed. It's that simple. If it was the other way around and a guard had died in a struggle it would have been murder. But when a prisoner or a 'patient' dies, it's made to look like some kind of unavoidable accident. Well let me tell you now, Michael died the day he arrived. He was slowly being killed by medication and everyone could see what was happening. He was being cooked alive in the Broadmoor ovens, sizzling away like a good old roast chicken. But he was a human. If he was an animal the RSPCA would have intervened and saved him. But we are just lunatics, and apart from family and close friends, who gives a flying fuck about the Broadmoor mad men? Do you? Well, you might just change your mind by the time you finish this book. But in the meantime, spare a thought for Michael Martin and his family.

I know it's a long time ago and I know that things change and move on. Maybe Broadmoor is no longer the sewer it used to be. But to me it is still and always will be Broadmoor, the number-one lunatic asylum. It can't be anything else. How can it be? It's got a hundred and fifty years of insanity behind its walls. Michael Martin was just one of many who never made it out of there, and believe me, even those of us who did still live with it. There is no escape.

We salute you Michael. Love and respect.

CHARLIE BRONSON

BROADMOOR –
A BRIEF HISTORY

Broadmoor. A two-syllable word capable of striking fear into the hearts of men and women alike, a name that can make the blood run cold. Today, it is one of three high-security psychiatric hospitals in England, but it still stands alone as the most foreboding and feared of the trio. With a hundred-and-fifty-year history of madness, its Victorian red brick bears down on new arrivals like an unbearable weight, striking terror and uncertainty into the most hardened criminal or madman.

From its earliest days Broadmoor experienced problems with how best to treat those it held, due to the hybrid nature of the clientele. Whilst the majority of asylum people brought to Broadmoor were fairly compliant and not an immediate threat (except for the index offence which had originally led to them being there), the transfer of dangerous and often violent men from the prison system meant that Broadmoor struggled with the administration and management of these two very different groups. Even today, the official website is keen to emphasis that Broadmoor is not a prison, stating:

> *Because of the outside appearance of the buildings, especially its high walls, and the inaccurate news reporting it has often received, many people believe that Broadmoor Hospital is a prison – it's not. Although most patients are referred by the criminal justice system, they are still patients in hospital and their daily routines and treatment programmes are designed to assist their therapeutic recovery.*
>
> www.wlmht.nhs.uk/bm/broadmoor-hospital

We will leave you, the reader, to form your own judgement on this when you read the account of a real-life 'patient' within the pages that follow.

Following the Criminal Lunatics Act of 1860, Broadmoor Criminal Lunatic Asylum was constructed in Crowthorne, Berkshire in the heart of rural England. The hospital was built to a design by Sir Joshua Jebb, an officer of the Corps of Royal Engineers, and covered an area of 53 acres (210,000 square metres) within its secure perimeter. The original building plans of five blocks for men and one for women was completed in 1868. A further male block was later added in 1902.

The first group of patients to arrive were ninety-five women in 1863, and the first of these was officially admitted on 27 May that year, for infanticide (murder of a child). The Broadmoor archives describe her as being 'feeble minded' and it has been suggested by modern doctors upon analysis of these notes that she was most likely also suffering from congenital syphilis. The original women's block was completely separated from the men's by a high wall, and had its own staff of twenty female attendants, although the medical staff were almost all men. The first male patients arrived on 27 February 1864, and in 1872 it admitted one of its first famous patients: Dr William Chester Minor, an American surgeon (see Famous Inmates, page 189). During World War I, part of Broadmoor was also used as a prisoner-of-war camp. Block 1 became 'Crowthorne War Hospital' and was used to hold mentally ill German soldiers.

From its inception, Broadmoor was managed by a Council of Supervision, appointed by and reporting to the Secretary of State for the Home Department. The Criminal Justice Act of 1948 transferred ownership of the hospital to the Department of Health (and the newly established National Health Service) and overall control to the Board of Control for Lunacy and Mental Deficiency (established under the Mental Deficiency Act 1913). The exterior of the building, with its increasingly higher outer walls and highly visible security features, saw Broadmoor become an imposing shadow on the landscape. With a large majority of the population coming from the penal system, many came to see Broadmoor as a prison.

Fear in the local community was to become deep-rooted when in 1952, child killer John Straffen escaped (see Famous Inmates, page 191). Within just two hours, he had strangled and killed five-year-old Linda Bowyer. He was recaptured before the day was out, but the consequences had already proved fatal. After the escape, the hospital set up an air-raid alarm system, which is still in place today. Tested every Monday morning at 10am, for two minutes, it is intended to alert people in the immediate vicinity and surrounding towns should any potentially dangerous patient escape.

One such patient had the opportunity to test the new alarm system when he escaped in July 1958. Leaving a dummy in his bed in something that resembled a scene from *Escape from Alcatraz*, Frank Mitchell cut through the bars of his room with a hacksaw, scaled an internal wall and then successfully negotiated the outer wall in what became known as a classic getaway. Luckily, no one was harmed on this brief excursion and it is documented that the superintendent – Dr Pat McGrath, who in 1957 had been appointed the tenth, and last, medical superintendent of what was still called 'Broadmoor Lunatic Asylum' – was keen to insist that search parties were not armed in their search for his missing patient.

The Mental Health Act (1959), which came into operation in 1960, again changed the name, this time to 'Broadmoor Hospital', calling it a special hospital for psychiatric patients '*of dangerous, violent or criminal propensities*'. However, the renaming of such a notorious building did little to quell the fears of the public, particularly those in the immediate vicinity, and Broadmoor was to come under fire again when in 1971, serial poisoner Graham Young (see Famous Inmates) was diagnosed as no longer a threat to the public and released. He went on to poison some seventy people at his place of work, fatally in two cases. He was sent to Parkhurst Prison, but the public were now asking why he'd been released and how the authorities had got it so horribly wrong.

Broadmoor was to see dark times indeed between the late 1970s and the 1990s, and remained under direct control of the Department of Health – amid reports of 'combined notional central control with actual neglect' – until the establishment of the Special Hospitals Service Authority (SHSA) in 1989. In July 1984 (see Introduction, page XVII) Michael Martin, a young black man who had been sectioned under the Mental Health Act (1950), died as a result of being restrained. He choked to death in seclusion, having been forcibly injected. Four years later, in August 1988, Afro-Caribbean Joseph Watts died as a result of a restraint operation to control him. With shields and helmets being used to hold him down, Joseph was forcibly injected. A subsequent report by the SHSA recognised that his religious beliefs had counted against him, and staff had often referred to Joseph as a 'gorilla' and 'monkey' and told him to stop going on about his religion or his medication would be increased. (Special Health Services Authority Report 1988, as cited in *Main Issues in Mental Health and Race,* ed. Ndegwa & Olajide, 2013)

It appeared that the resulting inquiries and investigations had done little to improve the situation, which seemed particularly daunting for young black men in Broadmoor. In August 1991, 31-year-old Orville Blackwood died of heart failure after being forcibly injected with a combination of promazine and fluphenazine decanoate. (Source: www.pb.rcpsych.org/content/18/4/236.full.pdf) A verdict of accidental death was returned at the inquest. An inquiry by the SHSA in 1991 made forty-seven recommendations for action and noted the similarities between the deaths of Michael Martin, Joseph Watts and Orville Blackwood.

By 1996 the SHSA had been abolished and replaced by individual special health authorities in each of the High Secure hospitals (Ashworth, Rampton and Broadmoor). A major inquiry into Ashworth Hospital in 1999 by Peter Fallon QC found, among other things, serious concerns about security and patient abuses resulting from poor management. It was decided that there had to be a review of security at all three special hospitals. Until this time each hospital was responsible for maintaining its own security policies. Sir Alan Langlands, then chief executive of the NHS (England), was given personal responsibility for the subsequent review. The report that came out of the review initiated a new partnership to be formed whereby the Department of Health set out a policy of safety and security directions that the three special hospitals should adhere to. These directions could then be updated or modified as necessary, and there would, in theory, be a sense of consistency across all three hospitals. Broadmoor's security systems were subsequently upgraded, from category 'C' to category 'B' prison standard, although higher levels of security are in place around certain buildings. New standards were introduced to increase security, as were procedures and equipment for reducing the amount of contraband smuggled into the hospital.

The Broadmoor Hospital Authority was dissolved on 31 March 2001 and West London Mental Health (NHS Trust) took over the responsibility for the hospital. A new unit called the Paddock Centre was opened in December 2005 to treat people diagnosed as having a dangerous severe personality disorder (DSPD). This clinical label of DSPD was a hotly debated topic, causing much disagreement among professionals within the field of psychology. The Paddock Centre was initially intended to hold seventy-two patients, but never opened more than four of its six twelve-bed wards. The female section of Broadmoor closed in September 2007, with the majority of the women moving to a new service in Southall, some to Rampton Secure Hospital and a few placed elsewhere in the mental-health system.

In October 2011, the Department of Health and the Ministry of Justice published the 'National Personality Disorder Strategy', concluding that the resources invested in the DSPD programme should instead be used in prison-based treatment programmes. The DSPD service at Broadmoor was then ordered to close by 31 March 2012. The patients were transferred either back to prison, on to medium-secure units to continue treatment, or to the residual national DSPD service at Rampton, with a few remaining in Broadmoor under a diagnosis of 'personality disorder'. Today, the Paddock provides admission and high-dependency wards for both the mentally ill and those deemed to have personality disorder, with seventy-two beds available. In total, Broadmoor holds approximately

240 patients. The average stay for a patient is five to six years and they are transferred to lower-security conditions once the risks they have posed are assessed as having diminished. The catchment area for the hospital now serves all of the NHS regions: London, Eastern, South East and South West.

Only those held within its walls can tell you whether they feel Broadmoor is a hospital or a prison, whether the conditions and systems documented within this book still exist. Sadly, for men like Michael Martin who had no voice, their cases are consigned to history, remembered only by those who loved and knew them, and perhaps those responsible for their untimely deaths. This book is written for Michael Martin, and his story, like so many others, is told for them by the experiences of fellow 'patient' Charlie Bronson. The reader may be relieved to know that along with what, at times, can be a harrowing story, Charlie has thrown in some anecdotal snapshots of life in Broadmoor, and the characters he met. There is also an informative section on Famous Patients, for the historians among you.

PART 1

BROADMOOR CRIMINAL LUNATIC ASYLUM

1979–84

CHAPTER 1

WELCOME TO THE LUNATIC ASYLUM

Fucking hell's bells. How did I end up in the maddest asylum in the world? Me! Me, of all people. How? Why? What the fuck went wrong? Who switched the light off? It's so hard to understand. So difficult to accept. So soul-destroying to fall in line. Why me? I'm not mad… am I? Could I really be insane? Did I deserve such a fate? How does a young man of twenty-seven face up to this crazy life? It's like waking up to a living, breathing nightmare. Bollocks to it. I can't live my life in this place with all these loonies, can I? Could you? Would you? Fuck it, I couldn't. Why should I?

I don't want to be mad. Prison's a bleeding holiday camp compared to this place. Broadmoor and me never mixed. It's not gonna happen, I'm not gonna let it. I'm gonna fuck this place if it's the last thing I ever do. Or it's going to fuck me. I'm not a fuckable type of geezer. You don't fuck with me. You might try, but you won't get far. You will get hurt… seriously hurt. I've gotta let this firm know that I'm not taking any shit here. Start off as I intend to finish, a winner. That's my goal. I'll walk out of this place a better man. A sane man, a man of respect, with dignity, and I'll keep my morals. It's game on. Time for fun. A walk on the edge, the dark side. It's bang on. Bronson v Broadmoor. Ding ding, round one!

Charlie's admission form to Broadmoor.

3 October 1979 – The Rampton van drove through the Hellmoor gates. Yeah, I had just spent eleven months in Rampton asylum. Another seriously godforsaken place. But that's another story for another time. This is the big house. An imposing red brick Victorian building, like in an historical adventure but with human monsters. There were seven Rampton guards in the van with me. As I jumped out, another ten Broadmoor guards were stood waiting for me. Seventeen men in total surrounding me, all of them as big as shit-house doors. The first thing that flashed through my brain was, 'Make sure you hit one before they smash the fuck out of you.'

It was the old routine, lots of eyeballing, weighing up, prodding and pushing, trying it on. 'What have you been up to, then?' one growled. 'We've heard about you. We tame lions here, so you can have it easy or hard, we don't give a fuck which way you want to do it.' They marched me off to Somerset Ward One, which was the reception block. Within five minutes I was in a cold bath freezing my nuts off. 'Hurry up, we ain't got all day,' a guard growled. 'Alright,' I said, 'hold your fucking horses.' He didn't like that. 'Oh, we got a tough guy here lads,' he said, looking round to his mates. It's a vulnerable position to be in, in a bath with ten nosey fuckers hovering over you like vultures.

'Nurses.' What a fucking joke. Let me explain something to you about these Broadmoor 'angels'. Apart from their white jackets, the uniforms are exactly the same as the prison officers. They've even got the size ten boots, and some of them are studded. They carry a bunch of keys, they chew gum, they walk like cowboys and they are fucking bullies. Bullies who stick together in the Prison Officers' Association, still calling themselves 'nurses'. Okay, not all of them. You always get a few humane ones doing a fair job. However, the ten clowns I've got surrounding me are what they are: bastards. They were dying to lay into a poor defenceless lunatic to show him who's the boss. One grabbed my arm to get me out of the bath. 'Fuck it!' I thought. Crack! My head connected perfectly. (My dad always taught me to get the first one in.) Unfortunately, with one down, it still left nine of the fuckers … the story of my life. So for my first day, I ended up in a cold empty cell with nothing but a cup of water, a smelly, lumpy old mattress and one indestructible blanket. Welcome to Broadmoor.

Mr & Mrs J Peterson
The Conservative Club
Eastgate Street
Aberystwyth   7347
Dyfed
                                    3 October 1979

Dear Mr and Mrs Peterson

Michael Gordon PETERSON

I am writing to let you know that your son was admitted to this hospital on Wednesday, 3 October 1979.

I enclose a copy of our booklet giving details of visiting times etc which I hope will be of help to you.

It is suggested that, initially at least, you should telephone the admission ward to find out whether your son is ready to receive visitors.

If at any time you change your address, I should be grateful if you would let me know.

                    Yours sincerely

                    for Physician Superintendent

Broadmoor's advice letter to Charlie's parents

The cell was approximately ten feet long, five feet wide and maybe twenty feet high. The window was blocked off by a wooden shutter with mesh in it, and there was no heating. It also stank of stale piss and the light switch was outside, so you had no control over it. It also had no call bell, which alone was illegal. Every prison and hospital cell has to have an internal bell in case of emergencies. But as I was soon to find out, Broadmoor has its own rules, *their* rules and there are no human rights inside Hellmoor. You do as you're told or you get what I just got, a very large injection in your buttocks.

I immediately felt drowsy, heavy and sluggish. My mouth was dry and my eyes were blurred. I collapsed onto the mattress and drifted away into a nightmare. When I woke up I was shaking. My teeth were rattling and I was both hungry and thirsty. I gulped down the water and had a piss in the plastic chamber pot. Then I heard it over the tannoy: 'Would Ron Kray come to the office?' My old mate Ronnie was here! He had arrived from Parkhurst Prison six months earlier and it was in Parkhurst that I had last seen the twins, Ron and Reg Kray. I felt great. About half an hour later I heard another announcement. 'Would Colin Robinson come to the office?' Fuck me, I couldn't believe it. Another of my old Parkhurst buddies. I'd known Robbo since 1974 when he got a life sentence. He got a second life term when he was up in Wakefield and attempted to murder a sex case. Robbo was eventually sent to Broadmoor because he had a weird habit of cutting himself and others, and swallowing things. He'd swallow anything, bedsprings, tobacco tins, nails, screws. But I loved the guy as a brother, so I was double happy to hear both his and Ron's name called out. I found out later that they had both been called to the office and asked if they knew me.

Soon after this, the guards came to see me. 'Both your mates are here and they are very settled. We don't need *you* unsettling them.

Are you going to behave?' They read me the riot act and told me all the Broadmoor rules. They told me that out of the twenty patients on this ward, half of them were very unstable and unpredictable. I said, 'Fuck me, they can't be as bad as you fuckers!' The guard had by now softened his growl. 'Look son, we started off on the wrong foot yesterday. Let's move on and get you up and mixing. First you need some clothes and to get cleaned up.'

So I was let out of the cell and off I strolled to the recess with my pot full of piss and them following me like a couple of dogs. It did go through my head to turn and sling the piss all over them but I actually needed a shit, so I emptied my pot in the sluice and dived into the cubicle for a crap. There ain't nothing in this world like a good shit. I've always taken pride in my health and fitness, and body movements. So when I shit, I feel blessed, because a good working body gets you through anything. I jumped in the shower to freshen up. 'Don't be long in there!' one of them shouted at me. Here we go again, they just can't stop themselves. I came out and one of the guards handed me a lock razor. This was to be the first shave in over a year that I did myself. At Rampton it wasn't allowed. The guards would sit you outside your cell on a chair and make you sit on your hands while they tore away at your face. I was never trusted with a razor, so it felt amazing to be able to shave myself. I was smiling as I did it. I was then handed some clothes. They weren't bad at all, and at least they fit. Not like at Rampton. At Rampton the trousers came up to my calves. It was all part of the asylum mentality, designed to belittle and humiliate you, to make you feel less than human. If you didn't look like a loon when you arrived, you fucking did by the time they'd dressed and shaved you!

I was marched into the day room where I immediately clocked Ronnie and Colin. I was buzzing. It was a wonderful feeling; I actually felt happy for the first time since I'd arrived. Robbo looked his usual mad self and he had recently recovered from a swallowing episode, but Ron didn't look too clever. He had lost a lot of weight and looked terribly gaunt, yet both men made sure I was sorted for goodies, giving me tins of salmon and tuna, chocolates and biscuits as well as teabags.

Now let me explain something to you about Ron. He was a schizophrenic who needed medication to stabilise his mood swings. Without his drugs he was a fucking serious problem. I'd seen him go absolutely berserk in Parkhurst, and I do mean insane; frothing at the mouth, eyes bulging, shaking in anger and almost ripping someone's face off. He put forty stitches in a Scouser's face just for looking at him the wrong way. He attacked a six-foot, six-inch guard once just for farting near him. Ron was a fearless man, but very dangerous without his happy pills. When that beast Peter Sutcliffe hit Broadmoor, Ron told him straight, 'Don't fucking look at me. When I walk in a room, that's when you walk out. Got it?' The Ripper knew not to argue with Ron. Fucking coward anyway, killing innocent women. I hope he rots in there till he's taken to the grave.

I believe at this time the Broadmoor doctors were trying out new drugs on Ron, to try and get a balance that would work for him. He just had that spaced-out look. All he did all day was smoke and drink tea. He seemed to be in a dream-like state. It's also no secret that Ronnie was gay and he used to disappear into the recess with a young loony. In fact Broadmoor was full of gays, some very dangerous ones. But I loved Ronnie like I loved my own dad. To be in his company was like sitting with royalty to me. I was a very lucky guy to share some quality time with him, 'cos fuck-all ever lasts with me. I can remember hearing about Ron's passing like it was yesterday, and fuck me, did it hit me big time. I woke like any other day on 17

March 1995 in Frankland Prison, ate breakfast and went out onto the exercise yard. It was a lovely sunny day, until I was told Ron had died. Well, he will never, ever be forgotten by me. ('*Madness is a gift of life. It's how you use it that counts.*' RIP Ron Kray)

Colin Robinson was also a tonic for me. Colin and me go back years. He is the original psycho. His eyes could melt ice. He had left behind a trail of destruction through his journey of institutions. This guy was a serious problem for the authorities. This was his second stay at Broadmoor, owing to the fact that they couldn't control him in any jail. So Broadmoor took him in to give the prisons a rest. He once cut up two sex cases with a razor. They lost so much blood they nearly died, and Colin was already serving two life sentences. He just did not give a shit. Believe me, you do not fuck about with men like this. Violence is a way of life to them. They live, breathe and dream it. You could argue that they are cold and heartless but I say, 'Don't fuck with what you can't handle and you're safe.' These types of men are in another world that the ordinary person can't possibly relate to, and you really don't want to.

There was a serious monster on Ron's block. I say a monster not just because his case was monstrous but because he actually also LOOKED like a beast. He had to be the ugliest bastard in the entire asylum. In fact he gave us Broadmites a bad name! One day a loon came over from Norfolk Block to Ron's ward and proclaimed that he had just smashed the monster's head in with a clothes iron. Oh well, ugliness is a gift of life to some. That battering only made him look worse, if that were possible. There is a lot of violence that goes on in the asylum that is just insane: unprovoked attacks and random acts from nowhere, just mindless and totally out of the blue. Like the day a patient bit into a fellow Broadmite's face and wouldn't let go. He was like a rabid, demented dog, hanging on for all he was worth.

He was dragged off and injected but the poor loon with half his face hanging off had to be taken off to hospital in an ambulance. It was just another day in the madhouse. There was the man who gulped down a bottle of disinfectant. Why? Who knows? I once witnessed a Broadmite jump over the canteen hotplate, pick up a full urn of soup and throw it all over the loons sitting at the nearest table. No one was able to establish why, I doubt he even knew himself. It's a lonely old existence, surrounded by madmen, never knowing what's going to happen next. You have to be on your toes at all times. Stay alert, be prepared. You have to be more prepared than a fucking Boy Scout if you don't want to be the next victim of a madman and his insanity. Old loons fall asleep in the chairs in the day room... easy pickings for a psycho on the prowl, looking for their next kill. That's why the patients like me would be useful; we would stop that sort of thing (well, any decent lunatic would!). I could never stand back and allow such cowardice to happen.

I think I'll take this opportunity to explain a bit about the ins and outs of the asylum world, which I am sure the reader will find amazing. For the purpose of this explanation, I'll stick to the induction ward, Somerset One. Somerset used to be called the Monmouth refractory block and it was only for the most disturbed loons. That all stopped one day in 1977 when Bob Maudsley and John Cheeseman took a third patient (David Francis, a convicted child molester) hostage and locked themselves in a cell, torturing him to death over the space of nine hours. Where the fuck were the guards? Nine hours it took them. When they eventually smashed their way into the cell, Francis was dead. His skull had been cracked open and a spoon was wedged in his brain. The new refractory Block was then converted into Norfolk Block sharpish. (Incidentally, Maudsley became known as 'Spoons' after that. Did he eat a piece? I don't know. Could he have done? You can bet your arse on it.) Maudsley was subsequently transferred to Wakefield Prison, where he killed two more inmates before eventually being shipped into 'Monster Mansion', the CSC unit at Wakefield. And fuck me, don't I know enough about that place?! But whilst we're on this subject of notorious inmates, let me tell you a bit more about some other famous Broadmites.

A strange and memorable case was that of **Barry Williams**. On 26 October 1978, Williams went on a gun rampage in his neighbourhood. He shot and killed five people, four of them his direct neighbours, as well as seriously injuring others who were lucky to survive the shooting. He was sentenced on 26 March 1979 and sent to Broadmoor. Having served fifteen years, he was released in January 1994 and placed in a hostel just six miles from the scene of his crimes. After a public outcry he was moved to a privately run residential home in North Wales. Local speculation suggested that Williams had changed his name, married and moved to Worcestershire. There was also a rumour that he had a child with his wife.

Well, Williams shot and killed five people at random. Why? For the fun of it. He loved a cowboy film. He was always first in front of the TV, right at the front when Clint Eastwood or John Wayne came on the box. I think he was just born in the wrong country and the wrong era. He would have fitted in well with Jesse James and his mob. That was his madness: he never fitted in with society. Anyway, it was around 1981 when I got to share a pot of tea with him and I asked him outright, 'Why did you shoot those five innocent people?' I looked into those black holes he had for eyes and he said simply, 'I don't know.' That day I was sure of one thing: 'That is one Broadmite who is gonna die in the asylum.' Well, how wrong could a person be? I wonder if he still has his trigger finger. It seems so because I heard they nicked him recently. They caught him red-handed with guns and a home-made bomb. [In October 2014 Williams was charged, under his new name of Harry Street, with possession of firearms and making an improvised explosive device, and detained indefinitely.] Fucking insanity at its best. The loon goes on a rampage, killing five innocent people, for no reason whatsoever, and he is let out after fifteen years. I knew it would only be a matter of time before the madness in him resurfaced.

They say there's more out than in – well, Barry Williams is definitely testament to that. Williams was probably the maddest fucker I ever met. He made Hannibal Lecter look like a pussycat. He served less time than I've spent in the strong box. It only confirms what I've known for years: the system is riddled with insanity. When Williams looked up at the night sky in the free world and saw all the beautiful stars above him, I wonder if he ever imagined he might end up back in Broadmoor. The slippery bastard worked his ticket to freedom, that's for sure. He must have a proper brown nose and the taste of shit on his tongue, that's all I know. The mind boggles. Oh well, it is an asylum.

Brian Donald Hume was another big Broadmoor character. Hume, a 29-year-old company director, was charged with the murder of London car dealer Stanley Setty. Setty's dismembered corpse was found in the Essex marshes in 1949. Hume pleaded guilty to being an accessory to murder but he was charged with murder and tried in January 1950. The jury, however, failed to reach a verdict and at his second trial the judge instructed the jury to find Hume not guilty. He pleaded guilty to the charge of being an accessory after the fact and received twelve years' imprisonment. He was released in 1958 and, knowing that he couldn't be charged for the same crime twice, he sold his story to a magazine in which he confessed to the killing of Setty.

In the same year he robbed the Midland Bank in London as well as the Gewerbe Bank in Zürich, Switzerland, going on to kill a taxi driver. He was sentenced to life imprisonment on 30 September 1959 and later, in 1976, he was judged to be insane and sent to Broadmoor.

Get on this. Hume also killed a guy and slung him out of a four-seater plane over the Channel. Real James Bond stuff, eh?! He served a few years in Switzerland, then got flown back here and stuffed in Broadmoor. He was a really nice chap actually, and I personally don't think he was mad. Dangerous yeah, criminally minded certainly – but not mad. I reckon he must be about ninety now, if he is still alive that is. He was knocking on a bit when I met him, his hair was greying and he had slowed down a lot in his nature and accepted his fate. But he was a nice chap.

That slag **Peter Sutcliffe**, the Yorkshire Ripper (see Famous Inmates, page 191) was sent to Broadmoor, thankfully long after I had left (luckily for him). My mate Ian Kaye stabbed his eye out. Now he's a one-eyed, fat, diabetic monster. Did you know women write him love letters? What sick bitches. Women who do that are worse than him. They're lunatics. Fourteen women he killed, and contrary to the media crap at the time, not all of them were prostitutes. Not that it matters what they were; they were innocent. Some of them were from loving families, good homes. How can any woman want to write to him, knowing that? It's a disgrace to womankind, doing that sort of thing.

Anyway, you can read more about the people in the Hall of Infamy in the Famous Inmates section, so let's move on. So here we are on Ward One of Somerset House and it's 1979. After only a couple of days I am witnessing things I don't believe. Things are happening before my eyes and I am finding it difficult to take it all in. It's insanity at its very best. Men laying down screaming, crying, shouting out for no reason and unprompted. The odd streaker, covered in shit with an erection most men would die for. Patients wanking away as they watch television in the day room. Loons swallowing table tennis balls, nutting doors and walls, cutting their wrists, attempting hangings. I saw men smashing up the place, stabbings, attacks. One guy jumped up on the pool table and shit on it, laughing as he did it. Our fucking pool table! I even walked in on a fucking sex orgy one day. Five loons at it, bumming and sucking each other off. Not a nice sight, believe me, especially before breakfast. One guy got rushed to hospital with six batteries stuck up his arsehole. Another loon attempted to drown a guy in the bath. One even chinned his own mother on a visit. I mean, if his own mother ain't safe, what hope have the rest of us got?! The day room was a hotbed of madness and I was trapped in there with the maddest of them all. 'I'M A CELEBRITY, GET ME THE FUCK OUT OF HERE!'

The average stay on Somerset was between three to six months, then you were allocated to the block you were gonna spend a good part of your life on. Maybe until you die, if you're unlucky. Both Colin and Ronnie were soon due to move on from Somerset. 'Fuck me,' I thought. 'I'll go mad without them.' I can't take all this shit on my own.' I actually started to feel uncomfortable. I didn't like it one fucking bit. I felt like Robinson Crusoe without Friday. Crazy. I was stuck in a room full of people but felt very much alone.

Ron was the first to get shifted, moving to Somerset Ward Three. Before he left he gave me one of his tins of salmon and tuna, and a good thirty giant bars of Galaxy chocolate. Ron was like that, very generous. I was saddened to see him move on and I knew that once Colin went, I would almost certainly flip. Colin had helped me fill in a lot of the spare time you find on your hands in Broadmoor. We played a lot of chess together, and cards and pool (until the loon shit on the table, that is). On one occasion a nut came over and started a load of madness, talking rubbish and trying so hard to fuck up our day. I grabbed him around the neck and squeezed hard: 'Now fuck off before I squeeze a bit too hard, you mad cunt.' I let go and he jumped me. Fuck me, he was all over me like a rash. I landed him a right hook and a few jabs. Goodnight! I got taken into the office and reprimanded. Did it end there? Did it fuck. The very next day he followed me into the recess and started again. I hit him so hard his whole body left the floor. Then I smashed his mad face into the urinal half a dozen times. Colin walked in on this and wanted to take the guy out. (Fuck me, get me out of here, I don't want to be here.) It was finished as far as I was concerned.

The loons who smoked were not allowed lighters or matches. (I wonder why! Oh yeah, some of them are pyromaniacs. They set fires and wank whilst watching the flames. The dirty pervs.) So there is a car lighter on the wall that they press and a wire lights their fag. Some were smoking forty, fifty, a hundred a day. The day room was always full of smoke; it looked like Victorian London at times. I was expecting Jack the Ripper to jump out. I actually got a bad chest because of it. It was very unhealthy to sit in there.

Anyway, eventually Colin was moved, which was inevitable, and my head went. I lost it. I was injected and went into a big black hole of a sleep. My life, my world was starting to drift into oblivion. I remember that it was around this time that I used to lay in bed laughing, laughing so much that it hurt. God knows why, but I just laughed. One night I started laughing and couldn't stop, and then others started, joining in with me. The whole fucking lot of loons were laughing behind their cell doors. It was totally insane. The night guards were kicking our doors, telling us to shut up and go to sleep. Twenty loons roaring with insane laughter and not one of us knew why. Welcome to the funny farm. I was crying with laughter. My ribs hurt so much I could hardly breathe. It was truly the maddest experience I can remember. I would say, admit even, that that night was the night I finally lost it. I fucking loved it. This was it. It can't get any better. I guess I had actually found myself in that moment of madness. The real me. The asylum had finally taught me the biggest thing I would ever learn in life: Keep on laughing. Be Happy. Always laugh. Don't let the place bring you down. Be one step ahead of their bollocks. Madness will help you overcome all of their hurdles. Be proud of yourself. This is the No. 1 hotel in the world. It don't get any better, it is magical. The magic house full of magic people. The guards only work here, we live here, this is our home.

As the old saying goes, 'The lunatics have taken over the asylum.' Well in my case I had, and I was about to make my mark. Broadmoor never could or would beat me, no way. I decided that very night that I would beat Broadmoor.

When my door unlocked the following morning, I walked out proud. Ten feet tall. I marched to the recess with a pot full of shit as naked as the day I was born, whistling 'Onward Christian Soldiers'. And would you believe, other loonies joined in with me. Colin had moved on and yet, I had found myself and I was reborn. Yarhoooo! Let's get this show on the road. I felt like I had woken from a long, wasted sleep. This was my haven, my new home. It's my party and I'll do what the fuck I want. You never know what's round the corner and nothing, good or bad, lasts for ever. Well, things were starting to look up. In walked two lads who were to prove a breath of fresh air: George Shipley and Michael Martin. George was from Feltham Borstal where they had been unable to control him, and little wonder. He was a proper handful, a typical borstal boy – in your face and he didn't give a flying fuck. He was full of tattoos, even on his neck and face. I liked George from day one. And of course there was Michael. Life was bearable and I felt good. That is, until a big fat nonce arrived.

This piece of dog shit came from Winchester jail. He was on remand there for killing his wife and four kids with a hammer. I instantly hated the sight of him. From day one he walked into the day room with his eyes to the ground. Shamed. He was a chicken in a room full of foxes. I went and sat next to him and whispered in his ear 'You fat, dirty, child-killing nonce…' I never expected him to jump up and run screaming from the room like a castrated pig. I never even touched him or got a chance to finish my sentence. What sort of man takes a hammer to his kids? The wife is one thing. Maybe she cheated on him (not that it's any excuse, but in jealousy people can flip in a moment of madness). But why four innocent kids? What had they done? Then I heard it. 'Peterson, come to the office.' My name sounded over the tannoy. It didn't take Columbo to work out why they were calling me. This was the very first time I was to meet the Medical Superintendent, Dr Patrick McGrath.

McGrath became the tenth and last medical superintendent in 1957 of what was then called Broadmoor Lunatic Asylum. He was a professor in psychiatry and had dealt with big cases over his thirty years, and I do mean big: the likes of Frank Mitchell, Ian Brady and other monsters you don't want to think of. In fact, he refused to accept Brady because he said Broadmoor could do nothing to help a sadistic murderer like him (well said, Doctor). I would have added, 'Hang the bastard, and that witch Hindley.'

McGrath was quite a friendly sort of chap, laid back, polite and respectful. He told me he had dealt with many prisoners and named a few – Roy Shaw, Frankie Fraser, Timmy Noonan, Marty Frape. He actually said he didn't really like to accept *my sort* (I'm not sure if that was a compliment or an insult). He then went on to explain why I shouldn't be nasty to the child killers! 'They are sick people, sent here to be helped and treated. Some have had serious breakdowns and it's my job to help them back to normality,' he explained. 'Broadmoor is full of sick people and you can't go around upsetting them.' Blah blah blah. It was the biggest pile of shit I'd ever heard. I said to him, 'Yeah? Like Straffen [John; see Famous Inmates, page 191] who escaped from here in the 1950s. He was in for strangling two kids. He then escapes and kills another kid. He should have hung and the third kid would still be alive today. It's all well and good saying these people are sick, try telling their shattered parents that. A child killer or paedophile is lower than a snake to me. Whatever you say to me, I can't but spit on the vermin.' And that was that.

He basically replied, 'Don't do it again or you'll be in trouble and moved over to Norfolk Block.' He thought this would frighten me. 'Ooh Norfolk,' I thought, 'please don't scare me. Please, please don't move me over to that nasty block.' Every fucking day I was told, 'You really don't want to end up in Norfolk.' I was sick of hearing about Norfolk. I actually said, 'Yeah? And believe me, they really don't want me over there either. Fuck Norfolk!' I'd heard about the feared Plastic Room in the Norfolk Intensive Care Ward. Well, us inmates called it that. It had a plastic window, a plastic bed; the mug, jug and dinner plate were all plastic, with a plastic spoon to match. It was a plasticated nightmare. You even started seeing things as plastic: the screws' faces would melt like a leper, into deformed plastic. It drove you insane. There were speckles of blood and blood stains on the walls, ceiling and rails. It was used as psychological torture, to instil fear into those who were stuffed in there to suffer. If you weren't disturbed when you went in, you certainly would be by the time they let you out. And yes, you guessed it – I spent more time than most in the plastic un-fucking-fantastic hell room. Bastards.

My time passed fast on Somerset Ward. My only real problem was the drugs they had me on. Enforced I must add, because I am totally anti-drugs. I was on a cocktail of Stelazine, Largactil, Modecate, Taractan and chloral hydrate [see Drugs Index, page 195]. Obviously I had no say in this; I took it voluntarily or it was forcibly administered. Fuck me, I rattled as I moved. I had some serious issues on all this shit. One of the worst of these drugs was Taractan, a disgusting red liquid they made me take. My whole nervous system broke down as a result of the combination of this shit. My first real bad attack occurred when I was behind a double-doored cell. Within half an hour of swallowing the red shit, my head was spinning. Fuck me, I thought it was gonna come off. My saliva dried up and my tongue felt like it was twice the size in my mouth. I couldn't see because my sight was blurred and the whole of my body was in agony. Then the terrifying thing happened: my spine and neck felt like it was bending and twisting up. I couldn't stand or sit as my body contorted into shapes you could never get yourself into normally. For a spell I refused to take it all, but then it all started. Steaming into my cell with a black leather mattress and smashing me up against the back wall, injecting me in the arse. I hated it. Then at medicine time I would have to open my mouth, swallow the pills and liquid and open my mouth and wiggle my tongue to show I'd taken it. I hated it.

By now I was totally unfit. I was four stone over my fighting weight. They were slowly but surely fucking me up big time. My family were disgusted with my unlawful treatment and shocked at my appearance. These drugs I was taking were for schizophrenics, manic depressives, psychotics, etc. I wasn't any of those, they were just using the drugs to control me. Abusing me and destroying me. I suffered blurred vision, muscle spasm attacks, night sweats, constipation, shakes, dryness of the mouth, headaches, pains in my back, restlessness. I was so tired and fatigued I slept almost all of the day as well as the night. I was one fucked up guy. My health was being destroyed by a bunch of cunts who knew I didn't need any of this shit. My doctor at this time was a Dr Tidmarsh. In fact it was him who had certified me mad in Parkhurst, along with Dr Cooper and Dr Falk.

In the Crown Court

at PORTSMOUTH

No. (N. 780076)

780670

on the 15th day of December 1978

MICHAEL GORDON PETERSON   (hereinafter called "the defendant")

has been convicted of wounding with intent
                        one and
And the Court has heard/(or considered) the (written) evidence of two medical practitioners (each) (one) of whom is approved for the purposes of section twenty eight of the Mental Health Act 1959, by a local health authority as having special experience in the diagnosis or treatment of mental disorders, and each of the said practitioners has described the defendant as suffering from   Mental Illness

And the Court is satisfied that the defendant is suffering from the following form of mental disorder within the meaning of the Mental Health Act 1959, namely,
                                            Mental Illness

and that the disorder is of a nature or degree which warrants his detention in a hospital for medical treatment and is satisfied that arrangements have been made for his admission to the hospital hereinafter specified within twenty-eight days of this date and that the most suitable method of disposing of the case is by means of a hospital order.

It is ordered that the defendant be admitted to and detained in   Rampton State Mental Hospital
                                                                   Rampton

And that the defendant be conveyed to the said Hospital by

Officers of H M Prison Parkhurst, Isle of Wight

(And it appears to the Court, having regard to the nature of the offence(s), the antecedents of the defendant and the risk of his committing further offences if set at large that it is necessary for the protection of the public that an order restricting his discharge should also be made.

It is therefore ordered that the defendant be subject to the special restrictions set out in section 65 of the Mental Health Act 1959 (XXXXXXXXXXXXXXXXXXXXXXXXXXXXXXXXXXXXXXXX) (without limit of time)).

And it is directed that pending admission to the said hospital within the said period of twenty-eight days the said defendant shall be detained in a place of safety, namely

H M Prison, Parkhurst, Isle of Wight

An officer of the Crown Court.

RM 1/72

Section Order used to send Charlie to Broadmoor.

Cooper was the PMO (Prison Medical Officer) at Parkhurst and Falk was a doctor from the Home Office. It takes three signatures to nut you off, and nut me off they did. However, 'I didn't have any faith in these head shrinks – as I don't now – and this indicates exactly why. Not one of the diagnoses of these three so-called 'experts' that certified me matched. One claimed I was a psychopath, another said I was a psychotic schizoid, and one couldn't make his fucking mind up whether I was a psycho or paranoid. Right now it didn't matter what the fuck I was, I was totally strung out on the liquid cosh [Largactil, see Drugs Index, page 195]. I used to bump into walls and doors, I'd lose my balance and I was always out of puff, for no reason whatsoever. My breathing was like that of an old man and my lungs were shot to pieces. I felt like a soldier who'd suffered mustard gas attacks. Fuck me, I was only twenty-six years old and I felt like a ninety-year-old. Surely I didn't deserve this. This wasn't treatment; it wasn't helping me. It was punishment, retribution and pure vindictiveness. Yes, I may have been a messed up young man, but I wasn't a murderer or a sex case. I'd lost my wife, my son, my family and my freedom. I may have been unpredictable and violent, but their treatment of me was just making me worse. When you're attacked, you fight back. It's human nature, and did I fight it! Well now, for the first time ever, I am going to tell you how I did it. In full detail. No holds barred. It's time to blow the lid on these bastards. Get on this.

Firstly, I drank eight pints of water a day. I pissed like a rhino, pissing out a lot of their shit, and in my cell I sweated a lot of it out. I would rip up a bed sheet and wrap my fists up, then stick the mattress up against the door and pound away. An hour of that and I began to feel alive. The wraps and the mattress would be drenched in blood, but it felt so good. The loons would be shouting 'Shut the fuck up!' while I pounded away. The guards would be kicking my door to try to shut me up. A couple of times they rushed in to inject me, all part and parcel of being in an asylum. But it didn't, and wouldn't, stop me, no way. I would be doing press-ups, sit-ups, squats and jogging on the spot, anything to sweat it out and keep my muscle strength. The walls of my cell would be dripping with condensation and dampness. It was airless you see, so there was nowhere for the air to escape. But I kept on and on and on. My press-ups became legendary (and they still are today). Even today at sixty-one years of age, I can smash out ninety-four in thirty seconds. That's not me being a bighead: it's a fact. I've worked hard to achieve it, such has been my determination. I used to do hand clap press-ups, deep press-ups, commando press-ups, one-arm press-ups, speed press-ups, slow dynamic press-ups. Sometimes in the day room I would get a loon on my back and knock out fifty press-ups (easy). But it was impossible some days. The drugs would be too much and I was fucked, tired and on another planet. Sometimes they gave me so much they just overcame me. 'Roll up, roll up, Smarties time, come and get it. Line up and wait your turn. Shuffle along, pull your tongue out.' Fucking cunts. It made me feel a deep hatred that has never left me.

Hey, what about some magical moments of madness that happened on this ward? You're gonna fucking love this. George Shipley went berserk with a pair of scissors and stabbed a fellow loony forty times. Fuck knows how he survived, but he did. That would cost George years of his life. He just lost it. 'Bang!' He was on a mission that day. He landed in Norfolk Block where he stayed for years. (Don't worry – I soon followed him over there. And Michael Martin. We were born for Norfolk.)

Then there was the time I was watching *Top of the Pops*. I'm sure it was Madness with their hit 'Driving in My Car' (fuck me, I wonder if they were on their way to Broadmoor!). A loon sat down next to me and just kept staring at me. I was starting to feel tense and agitated. It's not nice being stared at and, believe me, it's even worse when it's an unpredictable fucking loon in Broadmoor. I turned on him. 'Look pal, what's your problem?' He asked me if I would go to the recess with him and hit him. WHAT? 'Fuck off you loon. Get away from me.' Ron had warned me about this guy. Who the fuck wants to be hit, unless you're being paid for it? He asked again, so I decided to oblige his request. I said, 'Go to the recess and I'll be down in five minutes. When I got there, there he was waiting for me. 'Right, body shots or head shots?' I asked. He smiled and said, 'Head.' Bang, bang. He fell back and I caught him with a third shot. But as he fell back he smashed his head on a sink. Out cold. I dragged him over to the toilet and splashed some cold water on his face. As he came to he fluttered his eyelids: 'Ooh, that was lovely.' The mad fucker had no doubt shot his load. This loon was the first sexual masochist I met at Broadmoor. Fuck me, get me out of here, it's doing my head in.

Another of the loons would keep buying Smarties. He would pour them all into a bag and give them to me but keep the empty tubes. Why? I never asked. Why bother? I just loved the sweets. One guy swallowed a toilet roll. A whole toilet roll. How or why, don't ask. Another loon would shit his bed most nights and would come out in the morning covered in it. Not a nice sight, I can tell you. One nut used to read the Bible every day, upside down. Another lunatic accused me of killing his granny. She lived in Scotland and he thought I'd killed her in 1958. I was six years old in 1958 and I'd never been to Scotland. I still fucking haven't! (My head really hurts.) One took a swing at me in the dinner queue for no reason whatsoever. It just missed me. I ducked as he swung and as I came back up I caught him a peach of a right hook. It took him off his feet and I caught him again as he came down. To this day I'm not sure why he took a swing at me. I never stopped to ask.

One loon tipped his custard all over a guard without warning one day (we all cheered about that, I can tell you). Another day a loon jumped on a guard and bit his ear. He ended up in Norfolk Block (the loon, not the guard, unfortunately). One loon tried to rape another patient in the recess. His screams alerted the guards and they saved his virginity. One loon arrived without a cock; he had cut it off. Cut his own cock off. Can you believe that? Another turned up looking like the Elephant Man. Fuck me, he cheered me up. I couldn't stop looking at the ugly fucker. I used to throw peas and spuds at him in the dining room (he caught most of it in his mouth). One used to piss in the litter bin in front of everyone. One got a fork stuck in his eye by a psycho. The culprit was dragged straight to Norfolk Ward. One nut set fire to the library; he also went to Norfolk (best place for the madman). One desperate chap even superglued himself to a radiator. Nobody knew where he got the glue from. One attempted to escape by walking off a visit with a wig on. It was a mop head covered in black polish. Yes, it looked insane. (Well what do you fucking expect? This is an asylum.) One loon cut another loon with his dentures. It was one thing after another.

On the yard, most would sunbathe or just shuffle about like lost souls. Me, I used to jog, sometimes with a loon on my back. It was also around this time in my life that I started to sing. Dr McGrath told me it was a good stress reliever, to release pent-up emotion. You always feel better after a good blast. My favourite song was 'Onward Christian Soldiers' and some of the loons used to join in.

We were alive, living the dream. Well, nightmare, but we were living it big time in the big house, and don't you forget it. The grub was good, well cooked and there was plenty of it. They done a lovely fish and chips on a Friday and the Sunday roast was to kill for (Believe it! A hungry man is a dangerous man). But as I've said, with me fuck-all lasts. It was time to move. They had decided that I was to go to Gloucester Block. Some said it was a great move. I said, 'Who gives a fuck, let's go!'

CHAPTER 2

GLOUCESTER HOUSE

'Insanity is a way of life. Take it by the throat and choke it.
Enjoy the ride, strap in tight, it's gonna be very naughty.'

Fuck me, I had now landed bang in another world, a world I never knew even existed. This was medieval, Victorian, cuckoo land. This is where rocking horses DO shit. I felt my skin start to itch and sweat. From the second I walked into Gloucester Block, I felt lost as well as a strange sense of doom, like somebody had slung me into an abattoir to watch the slaughter. This was a very, very dangerous thing to do with a guy like me. Meaning, this was one challenge I did not expect. The tension in my body was like iron. Even my breathing was out of sync. All these old faces staring at me, dead eyes, the smell of despair, the pervading atmosphere of madness.

The corridors were called 'galleries', the cells were 'rooms' and the 'bedrooms' were 'dormitories'. Fuck me, not dormitories, surely not. They surely didn't expect me to live in a dorm. Not me. Would they? Could they? Am I being sent in like a lamb to the slaughter? All of a sudden I felt that any prison in the world would be heaven compared to this. Even the hard times in prison were a doddle compared to this shit-hole. I knew one sure thing: I was never going to survive much of this bollocks. They took me straight into the ward office and sat me down for a chat. It went a bit like this, and I quote:

'Now then, you are in Gloucester House. It is one of the best places for you. You'll be going into Dormitory Three.'

'Err, can't I have a cell?'

'No. A single room is a privilege and you have to earn it. It can take two to three years to earn a single room.' (Two to three years!)

'WHAT? Are you 'aving a laugh, you fat cunt? Who the fuck do you think I am, some sort of clown? Three fucking years in a dormitory with a bunch of loons. Get me out of here.'

The staff started to tense up as the atmosphere frosted over. 'Calm down. We don't want to start off rolling about with you. Just chill out.' There were six of them all stood there in their white coats, coiled and ready to pounce and jab me up. 'Now this is how it is ... blah blah blah'. I don't think I heard a word. I was just thinking of three years in a room full of mad axe men and baby eaters. Fuck me, I felt dizzy. I actually felt physically sick at the thought of it. They then showed me to the dorm I was supposed to be spending the next three years of my life in. It looked old, dusty and dirty. There were eight beds in it. I was later told my bed had been empty for a week. An old boy had died in it, so I was lucky as I had a new mattress. He was seventy-five years old and had died in his sleep, having spent forty-five years in Broadmoor. Maybe in forty-five years' time it'll be me not waking up.

'Right,' the guards said, 'we'll leave you to settle in. Oh, the medicine hatch is next to the office. Medicine time is 8am to 12am, and 3pm to 7pm'. I sat on 'my' bed for five minutes and I actually felt sad. It seemed to envelope me like a cloak. Fuck me, get a grip, I thought. 'Cheer up, it's not the end of the world, is it?' I said to myself.

I went to investigate my new home. Fuck me, it was eerie. I didn't like it one bit. I walked past some individual cells. One cell door was open and I clocked an old boy sitting on a large armchair. He was smoking a pipe. 'Hi son, come in.' And this was the first loon I met on Gloucester Ward. He was called Ernie Johnson. He was sixty-eight years old and had been a Broadmite for thirty-five years. He looked a lot like an older Ray Winstone, the actor. He was a proper character and I instantly liked him. He had come to Broadmoor during the Second World War for killing two men and had been in his cell for twelve years. It was his castle and it looked loved and lived in. From his window you could see Cornwall Block. He had old photos up on his walls and a big radio (a Roberts radio, the old-fashioned type with large knobs on it). He even had a goldfish and a budgie in the cell with him. He was so laid back and relaxed that as I sat and spoke to him I felt the tension draining from my body and my old self coming back.

He knew Frankie Fraser, Frank Mitchell and all the old legends of that era and his face showed that he had been through a lot of suffering. This was a man who had survived so much torture over the decades. I soon found out Broadmoor lived behind a wall of shame and fear. This place had carried out so much evil, you couldn't even begin to understand or comprehend.

Young men and women arrived here a hundred years ago, for *nothing*. Silly things like nicking apples, or being naughty, or setting fire to a haystack. How many of us can say we didn't mess around with matches or nick a packet of sweets as a kid? The worse we got was a clip round the ear. Did you know epileptics were even branded insane and sent to Broadmoor? Check out William Giles in the *Guinness World Records*. He came to Broadmoor as a ten-year-old boy in 1885. Declared an 'imbecile', prone to psychosis, he died in Broadmoor in March 1962 at the age of eighty-seven. His crime? He set fire to a haystack.

I soon began to learn the terrible truth about Broadmoor and its dark history. What lay hidden behind the imposing red brick walls. What horrors this building had hidden from the public, for not only years or decades, but centuries. The lobotomies, the electric shocks (ECT 'therapy', as they tried to call it), the decades of isolation, the brutality, the evil… I could go on and on. Libraries across the UK and the Internet are now full of the facts; you can research it for yourself. Finally the truth has started to emerge and it's not just the word of a madman against the establishment. This place was no better than a concentration camp, experimenting on the mentally ill and the sick.

All of the drugs they are enforcing on me are part of the experimentation, used for control. They weren't to try and 'cure' me because they knew I didn't have any form of mental illness. No one knows the long-term side effects but there are thousands of haunted men and women still suffering today as a result of the brutality they suffered at Broadmoor. For now, I am just a guinea pig, as is everyone else in this godforsaken place.

Do you know, I actually feel a surge of anger as I write this, some three decades later. Even now, I am locked in a maximum secure unit, isolated and kept in twenty-three hours solitary, but this is heaven compared to what I had there. Fuck it, I'm gonna stop here and have a cup of tea and calm down. I never realised that going back in my memory to that hellhole would reignite such emotions and frustrations as I feel now. I need a break. By the way, I was NEVER a psychopath. Psychopaths have no emotions or feelings of guilt. It's just a label they chose to give me and it stuck with me for many years afterwards. It was a misdiagnosis by incompetent doctors who didn't know what the fuck they were talking about. I was declared sane shortly afterwards.

As you'll learn, the authorities declare you 'mad' when they can't handle you, and sane when they want to hold you accountable for something, so they can nick you. Psychopathy is not curable, so if I was a psycho how could I suddenly be declared sane? It was shit, but shit sticks, like it does to a blanket. It's actually quite a shitty story, and the worst is yet to come. Believe me, you're gonna come with me to Hell. I want you all to bear witness to what I saw, experienced and everything I felt, and what I suffered alongside the poor souls in that place. You are about to become a Broadmite. But first I need a lie down. I will be back… and I will scare the shit out of you!

Okay, I am back. Now where was I? Oh yes, we were in Ernie's cell, weren't we? So there I am, having a cuppa and a chat with my new Broadmite friend. (By the way, I made that term up, 'Broadmite'. It sounds good, don't it? The Broadmite Firm. Broadmites rule!) Anyway, I finished talking to Ernie and had a little shuffle around my new home. Fuck me, it's spooky. I walked into the dining room and what hit me was the sheer size of it. It was massive, almost an underground cellar. These buildings were built on hills, the ground runs up and down.

Some of the loons were sat round, just staring into space like lost souls. One was knitting. Yes, knitting. He had long hair and looked like a hippy. I later found out he had killed his grandparents and gone off on a cruise. A very strange sort of chap. Cold and ruthless. There were some loons playing games (chess, Scrabble or Monopoly). It looked more like an old folks' home than the funny farm. The average age on Gloucester Ward was between forty and eighty, and there were a good sixty of us men on this ward. I would say that there were approximately forty of them that I couldn't ever relate to. They were just not my sort of people. They were weird, cuckoo and totally institutionalised.

One guy, Dennis Nash, was known as the Birdman. He had been in Broadmoor over thirty years and he bred budgies in an aviary out in the gardens. He was as gay as any gay ever! His whole character, his walk, his movements, his voice. It was a bit too in your face. He used the aviary to entertain the boys (I say boys, but not one of them was under thirty years of age).

The noises that came out of that bird shed were eerie; I found them disturbing. Looking back now I can laugh about it, but back then I felt quite strange whenever I heard them. It was not a nice feeling. It felt like I was trapped in with a pervo gang of loons. It was also no secret that one or two of the guards were regular visitors to the bird shed, and take it from me, it wasn't to stroke the budgies.

Dennis never once tried it on with me. He treated me with respect, as he liked ex-cons from jail. He had two sides to him, Dennis. One a raving fairy and the other a very serious character. One day he found out that his partner had cheated on him. He turned nasty and caved his skull in. He was sent straight to the dreaded Norfolk Block, staying there for years after that. As he was dragged away by six burly guards, all you could hear was him shouting, 'My birds, my birds. What about my birds?' I believe a local pet shop took them in and the aviary was stopped.

The garden, however, was a treat. Rockeries, flowers, there was even a little pond. I used to sit out there and I felt so good, so refreshed. It was almost like I was free. I used to analyse it all, taking everything in around me: the buildings, the people, the routines. Everyday life fascinated me. I would go into myself and imagine the 100 years of history here: the screams, the deaths, even the windows told a story. The faces looking out, peering down at me.

In Broadmoor there's always eyes looking. You are forever watched, scrutinised and constantly monitored. You are always observed and everything is documented. If you leave a fucking pea on your plate they write it in your file. They wrote a report on us every single day: your mood, your personality, dislikes, even what hand you wiped your arse with. Fuck knows what they found to write about me every day, but I was acutely aware that one bad report could result in my medication being increased to an even higher dose. It was enough to make you paranoid.

I became a great watcher myself. I was fascinated by the insanity surrounding me. I loved the unpredictability of people. A loon would shuffle out into the garden, snap a flower off its stem and eat it, and shuffle back in. Some would do strange, completely random things, like kneel on the grass and put their ear to it, listening for a while. I remember one old chap with silver hair came over to me and farted, laughed and shuffled off. I started to love these crazy people. The more I studied them the more I began to feel like I was a part of them.

Gloucester Ward had a full-sized snooker table and it was ours, the Broadmites, but the guards would always be playing on it, like the cunts they were. But they had to stop at some point. So I would wait for them to finish, nick a couple of balls and bury them in the garden. I bet someone was sat on a bench like I would frequently be, watching me thinking, 'What's that loon doing burying snooker balls?' Eventually I got a tug, and was pulled into the office. 'Where's the balls?' the governor asked. I looked fazed. 'What balls?' 'Look, it's only since you came here that the balls have started going missing. So where are they?' I shrugged my shoulders. They never did find them. They must still be there. I wonder if anyone ever found them all.

Well, my first night in the dormitory was a night to remember. I bet you're dying to know. Hey, I'm dying to tell you. Well I wasn't happy, I can tell you. I felt uncomfortable among these loons in an open room at night. Who were these maniacs? What had they done to become Broadmites? You try sleeping in a room with a bunch of lunatics, not knowing what their crimes are. Was one planning on cutting my throat? Was one waiting for me to fall asleep so he could strangle me... and shag me up the arse as he did it?! This is Broadmoor, not Butlins. This is very thin ice to me. I did not like this set up one bit.

So there I am, there WE are, all ready for bed, in our cosy little dorm. I always sleep naked, so I stripped off and jumped into bed. I lay there watching. Some had pyjamas, some were naked like me. All of them were unfit, with big bellies and fat arses. Not their fault of course – it was years of drugs and the inevitable laziness that sets in. Then the farts started, loud and plentiful. Fat people do fart a lot, they can't help it. But that's no consolation to me. The room stank of stale air and gassy farts. Then one would be bashing his meat under the covers. Another was coughing, and one got up to go to the toilet, walking past my bed naked with a hard-on.

Fuck me, I'm sick of this already and it's my first night and I haven't even fallen asleep yet. But others had. Then the snoring started. Some were already talking in their sleep. How the fuck can I sleep among this bollocks? I'm bored now. I got up and went over to the loudest snorer. I picked his bed up at the end and slammed it down. Up, down, up, down. Up, down. He bolted upright in the bed. I punched him straight in the face. 'SHUT THE FUCK UP!' Other Broadmites woke up and are now looking at me, the new loon on the block. 'SHUT THE FUCK UP, YOU LOT OF CUNTS!' I shouted out. Later that night I had to get up for a piss. I was half asleep as I shuffled to the toilets. BANG, I am faced with a loon right up the arse of another loon, pumping away like a demented dog. I felt so defeated. They both smiled at me like it was a totally normal and natural thing to be doing in the middle of the night in a toilet, in an asylum. I took a piss and made my way back to bed, drifting off into my own hell. Why me? What have I ever done to deserve this?

Throughout the night the guard watchman would do his rounds every hour. It's crazy really because once he does a round, it gives the loons an hour to get up to whatever they fancy, and banging arses was the top hobby for some of the Broadmites. They loved it. Now I know why some of them walked funny. (Hey, come on, you've just gotta love these loons, they do grow on you.) The guy I had hit in the face woke up with a beautiful black eye in the morning. He looked like a panda. I got a serious pull off the guards for that. I knew one sure thing as I stood in the office that morning: I would not be living in Gloucester Block too long. That was the one thing I knew. And boy, how right I was.

Let me explain for you the layout of Broadmoor Asylum. I really should have described this at the beginning (better late than never, folks). Broadmoor consists of eight Victorian houses, all three-storey blocks. These are named the following:

1. *Norfolk Block*
2. *Essex Block*
3. *Kent Block*
4. *Dorset Block*

5. *Somerset Block*
6. *Gloucester Block*
7. *Cornwall Block*

Hang on a minute, you say, that's only seven. Yes I know. (No fear, you haven't caught me out). In fact, this is a bit of a trick question I ask people who tell me they have been to Broadmoor. How many blocks does Broadmoor have? Most say seven. Ahhhh, but what about Block 8? There is an eight, and the guards were famous for threatening us with it and rubbing it in our faces. 'You'll end up in Block 8, you will.'

Block 8 is the Broadmoor cemetery. They call it the last stop, and it is full of bones dating back a hundred and fifty years. Let's face it, the majority of Broadmites were disowned by their families (especially back in the Victorian days when mental illness had such a stigma attached to it). Lots didn't even have families. They had nothing and nobody. Landing in Block 8 is a pauper's burial. I suppose nowadays it's probably different, but in my days at Broadmoor, you ended up in Block 8 if you had no family to bury you.

There are also two other blocks, York Block and Lancaster Block. They are the pussy dolls houses, for the Broadmite Bimbos. Well, you do get loony ladies too! Where do you think they go? I'll tell you where: Broadmoor. On a windy day you can smell the pussy. Honest!

So where were we? Oh yeah, Gloucester Ward, and I am quickly becoming bored of the place already. I end up chinning a loon in the dining room. He was upsetting me as I was eating a meal. I told him 'Behave…' twice! He kept on, so I hit him. Bang, lights out. I'm taken to the office for the same old bollocks. Now I am even more bored, so I get up to leave. I am jumped on by a good eight guards and dragged off to an empty cell, where I'm forcibly stripped and

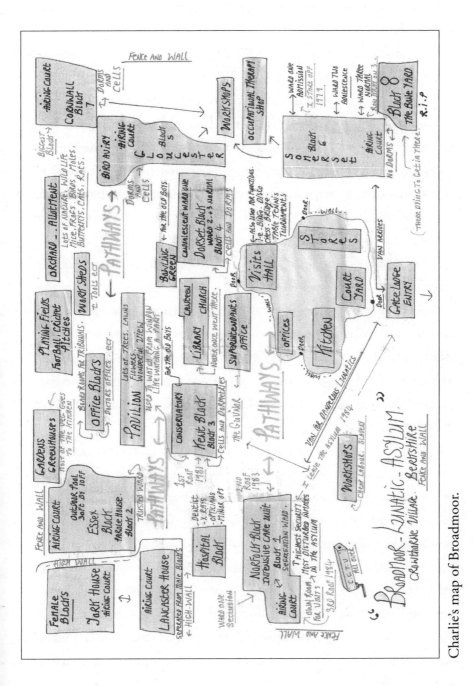

Charlie's map of Broadmoor.

injected in the arse. Night-night. I'm in Disneyland. I am out of it for a good twenty-four hours.

When I wake up I have a throbbing headache and my body is black and blue all over. They come back in to me. 'This is your final chance or you're off to Norfolk Block. And by the way, where's the snooker balls?' They never let up, do they? (Fuck 'em. Try playing snooker with no balls, you muppets! They're like a bunch of grannies at a bridge class). I'm now pacing up and down the galleries and I am angry, bored and feeling dangerous. I pop into old Ernie's cell for a chat. 'Cor blimey, you look tense, son. Come in, have a cuppa.' He said that he could see I didn't like it here and explained that neither did he when he arrived. 'But it grows on you, it's not so bad. Chin up.'

I poured out my frustrations to him. 'Look Ernie, I cannot handle this shit. I can't even get a good night's sleep. It's driving me mad. I am on the edge. This train's gonna derail and crash because I am fucked up big time.' He tried to reassure me. 'You'll get used to it. Give it a try. You don't want to end up on Norfolk Ward with nothing.' Fuck me, I had nothing already.

I went for a bath to try and have a soak and relax. They had no showers here, too modern for this antiquated place. Somerset Block had showers but here on Gloucester it's a wonder they even had electricity. You could still see the gas lamps on the walls that had been used to light the corridors. All the cutlery still had the initials BCLA inscribed on it: Broadmoor Criminal Lunatic Asylum. The Mental Health Act of 1959, which came into operation in 1960, changed the name to Broadmoor Hospital. They can call it what they want – it's the nuthouse and always will be. Nineteen years later and we were still eating with the same fucking knives and forks and they're trying to convince everyone this is a hospital.

Anyway, I am soaking in the bath and this lunatic creeps in and slings a boiling jug of water at me and runs out. No reason or motive. The loon probably just thought it would be a bit of fun to leave me looking like a fucking leper with skin dripping off my face. Luckily the cunt missed me. But he'd just made the biggest mistake of his life because I clocked his face. I jumped straight out, dried myself and got dressed. Now I am on a mission. Can you believe he had run into the office and asked them to lock him in the seclusion room?

I'm now looking in at the coward through the peephole. You little cunt. I was seething. Scald me will you, you little snake? Guards came over and moved me away from the door. They've asked me what the problem is. 'Nothing,' I replied, walking off. I am fuming. My doctor, Dr Tidmarsh, calls me to see him. He tells me that he realises I am not settling in too well. 'I'm okay, I'm cool.' Why did I say that? I'll tell you why. You learn to tell these people fuck-all. Anything you tell them will be twisted and used against you. Believe me, I've had forty years' experience of their bollocks. Right now I am on one. Enough is enough; this is payback time. This locomotive is about to smash bang into Gloucester like a hurricane. It's on. Every guard, every doctor, every Broadmite from this moment on is a target – except for the old legends, I wouldn't harm them 'cos I love 'em. Deep down in my heart I guess it's how I see myself ending up: an old, lost, insane man. But right now I am far from being in Block 8.

I collared a kitchen worker called David Francis and asked him to get a knife, snap the blade off the handle, bury it in a large potato and leave it for a few days until the heat was off.

The deal was I would repay him with five packets of fags. My plan was simple. I was going to tie the blade on a broom handle like a spear and go on a mission of madness. I had been driven to this and I now felt that it was 'get it first, before some bastard takes me out'. I

BROADMOOR HOSPITAL

INCIDENT / CASUALTY REPORT

SERIAL A: № 710

| Date of Incident / Casualty | 9/1/80. | Time of Incident / Casualty | 8·15 p.m. | Location | Gloucester. W.11. |

Name(s) of Patient(s)	Hosp. No.	House	Ward	RMO
PETERSON. M.	7347	Gloucester	II	DR. A. Tidmarsh.

Description of Events leading to Incident/Casualty *S/E/N Coshell informed by Patient that this patient had asked him for a knife for the Main Kitchen so that so that he could 'steal' a staff he so that he could have a proper 'Killing' of it this time. R.M.O informed and ordered seclusion until do and time as so by her. Secluded at 8.30 p.m. p.p. Day Report. No trouble. M/n T Walden (M/o Admin) informed.*

Description of Incident/Casualty and extent of any Restraint used

NIL

Witnesses to Incident	Discipline	INDIVIDUAL REPORT ATTACHED YES/NO	Signatures of Witnesses
S/N. D.O. SMITH.	S/N.	No.	D.O.Smith
S/N M. Coshell. Present with me later	S/E/N.	No.	M Coshell

Injuries sustained by Staff : NIL.
Patients :

Damage caused to Property : NIL.

How was Incident Resolved : *Placed in seclusion*

Signature : MO Attending _____ RMO _____

Senior Staff on Duty : _____

Discipline : *Charge Nurse.*

M.81

Incident Report Form regarding the knife Charlie tried to procure.

paid the loon his 100 fags and an hour later I am jumped on, injected and dragged over to Norfolk Block by the gorillas calling themselves nurses. I'd rather have Beverley fucking Allitt looking after me. Remember that evil bitch? She was done for murdering four babies and injuring scores of others. She was supposed to be caring for them, a nurse! I'm surprised she didn't get a job in this hellhole. But right now anything would have been better than these thugs climbing all over me.

On arrival at the dreaded Norfolk Block, I was very drowsy, practically out of it, but even now I can vaguely recall the reception I got. A good dozen guards all in white coats were manhandling me, pushing and shoving me this way and that. There was the odd punch and kick here and there, and plenty of verbal threats. 'You're gonna die here, Peterson', 'You're a worthless piece of shit.' Nasty fuckers! I was slung straight into a cell with just a mattress on the floor. I remember a face, inches away from mine, snarling at me, and a hand squeezing my neck. 'Listen you cunt, you're now in Norfolk. You do as you're told. Any fucking about and you're in for it.' The door slammed and the light went off in my head. I drifted off into the familiar big black hole and I remember thinking, 'I hope I never wake up.'

CHAPTER 3

NORFOLK INTENSIVE CARE UNIT

'This train ain't stopping. It's a one-way ticket.
You don't ever return. Say goodbye to your sanity!'

Well, I did get my single cell, after all! They could stuff their dormitory right up their arseholes. Here I am in the feared Norfolk Block and I have to say, it's not been so bad up until now. Silence is wonderful, but in the land of cuckoo it never lasts long. Wow, I am aching. As my senses slowly return to me I realise that my whole body hurts. My eyes feel blurry and tired, my nose is swollen, my lip's cut. I then notice that a couple of my toenails are missing. Suddenly I'm not feeling too well, I feel like I've crashed. The door smashes opens and they are back. The Norfolk Mafia.

''Ere y'are, get these down your neck.' I ask what they are. 'Pills. Your doctor prescribed them. Take them or you'll be injected.' I knew I didn't have the strength to fight at this stage, so there was no point adding to my injuries. I swallow the four pills, gulping them down with water. Fuck knows what they were. They could have been cyanide for all I knew. They pass me in a plate of beans on toast and a mug of tea and all of them traipse back out. SLAM. I'm alone again.

I sit on the mattress to eat and the warm food feels good. I roll over and slip back into sleep. I feel a strange sense of comfort, strange considering such cold and harsh conditions. This is better than having to live surrounded by loons, with so many obstacles in my way. I much preferred this. A solitary existence. A bit of peace. Time to reflect, get some rest and enjoy a deep sleep.

I was woken up when the door swung open again. Dinner arrived. It was the same routine over and over, like fucking Groundhog Day. Eat, drink, sleep. Pills, eat, drink, sleep. Pills. Pills. Sleep. Eat. Shit. Sleep. Eat. Pills. Piss. Shit. Sleep. The crazy thing was I had to shit and piss in a pot, and they would come in and take it away to empty it. What a job! Fucking turd collectors. I had a week of this bollocks. A whole week of nothing, complete nothingness. They said I was too dangerous to be let out in the exercise yard, despite the fact that it is illegal to deny a prisoner (sorry, 'patient') an hour's basic exercise a day.

My cell was approximately twelve feet long by six feet wide. The door was made of solid oak and in the wall by the door was a hatch that opened to pass in – yes, you've guessed it – pills and water. Through this hatch I would watch Norfolk life pass me by. Loonies walking by, slopping pots out, food trolleys passing, guards walking past. Everyday life unfolded before my eyes and it amazed me. My window had a big shutter on it, so I couldn't see anything and the air was stale. The walls were bare except for the many speckles of blood. There were speckles on the floor too. Some poor bastard had got it in this cell, I knew that much. Now it was my turn.

I wasn't allowed books, papers or anything to read, or anything to write with or on. I had nothing except my own space and my own time. Just me and an empty room but, strangely, I felt happy, contented. If it hadn't been for the drugs, I would have felt elated. Solitary to me is a walk in the park. You become your own man, your own master. I decided to start a routine and to stick to it. Time became meaningless. Who cares about time? I would walk up and down for hours, hop, skip, jump, jog on the spot, anything to keep my legs strong. I would do my press-ups, squats, star jumps, all sorts to kill the time.

Weeks soon turned to months. The guards get to know you in the end. It's unavoidable, they see more of us than they do their own wives. Often they would do twelve-hour shifts, fucking overtime grabbers. They used to live on *our* food, always nicking the best chop or chicken leg. Greedy, lazy cunts. They soon got fed up of me shouting and banging on the door at meal times. 'Oi, leave our grub alone!' Soon after that my portions seemed to go up in size, just to shut me up. Some of the guards actually came to understand and like me. Those that I can remember who treated me well were Clive Mason, Roger Russell, Tim Frampton and Stuart Elliott. Others just remained cunts. A cunt's a cunt in my book and always will be. There's no changing them.

Unfortunately, my doctor now was a Doctor Loucas. Believe me, this was very fucking bad news, for anyone in Broadmoor. It was only later in his career that he was exposed for the evil swine he was. In December 1992, Shadow Health Secretary David Blunkett raised a question in the House of Commons to the Secretary of State for Health, Virginia Bottomley. He asked what plans she had to investigate allegations of professional misconduct by Dr Kypros Loucas and said, 'I find these allegations very disturbing. Why was this man allowed to work within the official system up to seven years after these allegations were first made?' (http://hansard.millbanksystems.com/written_answers/1992/dec/10/dr-kypros-loucas#S6CV0215P0_19921210_CWA_308)

Loucas was a Greek Cypriot and a flash little fucker. I hated him and *still* hate him today, whether he is alive or dead, and when the facts are revealed, you will understand why. We had some serious blow-ups – and I do believe he hated me. He must have, to have done what he did to me. With him as my doctor, my drugs were DOUBLED, which made it hard for me to work out in my cell. His way of winning was the injection and he was famous within Broadmoor for using ECT, the shock treatment.

In December 1992 a Channel 4 *Cutting Edge* documentary entitled *Special Treatment* was shown, alleging that Dr Loucas had breached the Mental Health Act (1959). According to documentation later sent by Commission Members to Broadmoor and the Department for Health, Doctor Loucas *'sometimes failed to seek patients' consent for treatment when the act stipulated that he should have. He also failed to seek second opinions on some patients' treatment when those patients refused or were unable to give their consent... Sir Louis Blom-Cooper, Chairman of the Mental Health Commission, says it was particularly concerned that Dr Loucas was failing to make available documentation concerning the treatment of patients, which commissions were entitled to inspect.'* (*Independent on Sunday*, 6 December 1992)

Lord Colville, then Commission Chairman, stated that it was questionable whether Dr Loucas's patients were receiving the protection that the Act was intended to confer, if their consent was in doubt. (*The Independent*, 6 December 1992).

Further allegations came to light when a former student nurse at Broadmoor said he had witnessed Dr Loucas give unmodified ECT ('unmodified' meaning without a muscle relaxant) to a disturbed patient who was in isolation and behaving violently.

The makers of the documentary also obtained a signed statement from a former patient who stated he had been given unmodified ECT. He alleged that '*Dr Loucas got the staff to hold me down and then he would shout "Let go!" at the last minute and flick a switch. I had 17 lots of ECT like this.*' (*Independent on Sunday*, 6 December 1992)

Dr Loucas was eventually asked to take early retirement. By the following year he was working as a locum consultant psychiatrist at Horton Hospital, Surrey. It came to light that his appointment was via Dr John Wilkins, who had worked at Broadmoor during 1985–86. Loucas had had no formal interview and references were not taken up.

After this post he moved to HMP Wormwood Scrubs. The Home Office said the prison '*was aware Doctor Loucas had been asked to take early retirement from Broadmoor, but that it had no cause for concern about his clinical performance.*' (*Independent on Sunday*, 6 December 1992) His employment at Wormwood Scrubs was terminated with effect from 22 March 1993.

Loucas used to threaten me with ECT, but he knew he would never have gotten away with this. A lot of the patients had no family but I did, and they would never have stood for it. It was supposedly meant to be used for chronic depression. But I saw it for what it was: torture, no more, no less. I'd seen some of the loons being wheeled in for ECT and when they were wheeled back out, they were motionless. There would be blood and shit on the sheets. The trolley looked like something a wild animal had attacked. One day they did it and this poor bastard bit his own tongue off. They had way too much power, with no one to answer to, and it was serious abuse.

I was by now having serious side effects of my own, being given way more medication than was necessary. I was having blackouts and began suffering dizzy spells and heart palpitations. But worst of all were the neck and spine spasms. It was pain like I had never experienced before in my life, and never have since, nor do I wish to have. My spine would suddenly seem to bend like a bow in the opposite way. My neck would twist and fall onto my shoulder. It terrified me. Whenever it happened I would think to myself, 'This is it, I am stuck this way for ever. I'll be a cripple.' I cried unashamedly in agony as some of these attacks happened. I was actually being tortured, but for what reason? What purpose? It was making me so angry and bitter. There was no logic to it, but Dr Loucas refused to take me off of the pills. How could he ever call himself a doctor? He wasn't treating the patients, or helping us; he was simply containing and controlling us.

I'm going to confess something very personal now, and this is not the sort of thing a man will own up to easily, but I feel it needs saying, to explain to people what these drugs were doing to me as a young man and why I felt so bitter. My wanking days stopped. I could no longer shoot my juice. That alone was a major worry for me. It actually scared me. There was just nothing there. I was all dried up. Washed up. Now perhaps you can understand why I got so angry.

When my door eventually opened one day, a guard bellowed at me, 'Out you come, you're getting a shower and some fresh air.' I walked out and jumped, no, DIVED on one, attacking them. I was soon grabbed and smashed back into the cell, and quickly jabbed up. I don't know fully why I did it, but it just felt like a surge of pure hate. I could not control it. I really was a Broadmite now. I was lucky this wasn't the forties or the fifties, because I suspect I would have been given a lobotomy. I just felt like I had no more to lose in life and I didn't care anymore. Don't get me wrong, I don't mean that I was suicidal or had thoughts of this nature. I just thought, 'Who cares about the real world?' This was now my world. I was a true Broadmite now. A real madman in their eyes.

It's not easy coming to terms with who you are and what you have become. It's not easy to accept such an ending to your life, but it's what I had become, through my treatment and years of abuse: A very unpredictable, dangerous man. I felt a strange feeling of indignation, like 'Right, I am ME. Who are you?' If it wasn't for the few decent guards I have already mentioned, believe me, I would have been a hundred times worse. They sort of helped me keep a lid on it a bit. 'Oi, pack it in. Leave him alone,' they would shout out when it looked like trouble was brewing. These few good men were basically on my side, stopping further confrontations and I knew this. Perhaps it was more for their own sakes and safety than mine. They wanted an easy life and to return home of an evening with their faces still on! But it's like they say, if you keep on prodding a bear in a cage it will eventually rip your arm off. It's only natural and us human beings are the same.

So I started to go out on the court (they called it an airing court). It was about fifty feet square and surrounded by a twenty-five-foot wall. I would be allowed to go out there, alone, in my pyjamas, slippers and dressing gown. I had no clothes by this stage as they decided I was not allowed them. The only time they would give me clothes was when I had visitors, and all of my visits were held in a small room in the Norfolk Block.

My visitors at this stage of my journey were my mum and dad, my two brothers John and Mark, my sister Loraine, aunties Pam and Eileen, uncle Jack and Ian and three to four close friends (Johnny Bristol, Dave Taylor and a few others). Mike, my son, was by now ten years old and I hadn't seen him for seven years. My ex-wife Irene had remarried and it was all so far behind me I felt like it had never happened. Anyway, it was best this way. What son needs it in the playground? 'Your daddy is a lunatic! Loony, loony, loony.' Mike didn't need that to grow up with, he was better off without me. Sure it hurt. It fucking crucified me when I let my thoughts turn to it. But if you let thoughts like that chew you up, you'll be swinging from the end of a rope before the day is out. Meanwhile, Mum and Dad were disgusted at my treatment. They could see the deterioration in me every time they visited. The drugs were now the biggest part of my world. Without them I shook like an old man with Parkinson's. Even with them, I shook. I was a total fucking mess.

There is one night that I can never erase from my memory and I will share it with you. I got out of bed to have a shit. As I sat crouched on the pot I must have fallen asleep 'cos when I awoke, I was stuck to the fucking pot. The air suction had stuck it on my arse and I couldn't get the poxy thing off. I was like one of those crabs with the shell on. I gave up and went back to bed in the end, with the pot still stuck on my arse. The guards had to get it off the following morning.

It was around this time, November 1982, I started getting excruciating pain in my left ear. The pain was constant and had started to affect my jaw and neck. All I had for weeks was a throbbing sensation. And for weeks I kept telling them that something was wrong with me. I felt like I was being driven berserk with the pain. But this is Broadmoor, remember? And I was stuck in the dreaded Norfolk Ward. They liked to call it the 'Intensive Care Ward'. Ha! It was a punishment block and we all knew it. A pure hellhole. And I was stuck in isolation in the shit-hole. My good pal Lord Avebury was concerned for me and was writing to them, but that slag Dr Tidmarsh replied and told him I was doing fine!

23 - 4 - 82

Dr Tidmarsh

Mick Peterson 73478
NORFOLK PUNISHMENT BLOCK
ISOLATION WARD !

THANKS FOR TELLING LORD AVEBURY I'M
COMING ALONG OKAY, MUST BE ALL THE
SOLITARY CONFINMENT,

YOU SURE NO HOW TO TREAT US
PRISON LADS,

LOCK THEM BEHIND A DOOR,
AND FORGET THEM !

Thanks for Mathews

Micky Peterson

"PS" SOME TREATMENT

Charlie's letter of complaint to Dr Tidmarsh.

If you still think it's a hospital, get on this. These places always put security above the health of the inmates. You could die before they would allow you out to a real hospital to get tests or treatment. I asked to be taken out to be examined and for weeks I waited, in fucking agony. If it had been a brain tumour or cancer I could have died there and then. A Broadmoor doctor eventually and reluctantly came to see me in my cell. Did he enquire what my problem was, or investigate it? Did he bollocks. He just stuck something straight into my ear, violently. All hell broke loose. I lost it. That was it for me, the final straw. I jumped on him, more out of pain than anything else.

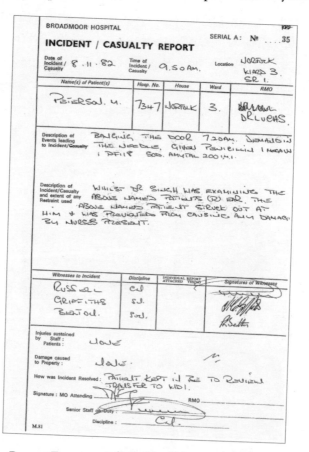

Incident Report Form regarding Charlie's ear problem.

The situation was quickly calmed down and no one was hurt, although I was still in agony and I knew my problem hadn't been solved. The guards promised to listen to my pleas for a transfer to hospital, so I could be checked out. I was eventually told I was going to be taken to Central Middlesex Hospital on 3 December. A whole month had passed but finally I felt like I was going to get to the bottom of whatever my pain was. However, I should have known it wasn't that simple. This is Broadmoor, remember. I was informed that my scan had been cancelled.

Some evil swine of a doctor called Dr Udwin had vetoed my hospital visit on the grounds that I was planning to escape. Where the fuck this had come from, I'd no idea. Apparently I had been discussing with NURSING STAFF (the guards) the possibility of escaping during the trip. You couldn't make this shit up. I almost didn't believe it, but I had the proof in writing because my good friend Lord Avebury was on to the case. I might have been declared insane, but I'd have to be fucking retarded to do such a thing as this.

One of Charlie Bronson's drawings from his Broadmoor days.

ROUTE FORM

......M. PETERSON................
(Name)

.. ..7347/N1 ....
(Hospital No. and House)

On ..Friday 3 December........ 19 82... the above named patient

will ....attend the Central Middlesex Hospital, Acton Lane,....

..........LONDON NW10..for.C.A.T. Scan at 12 noon,..................

....

....

He will leave Broadmoor at ..10.30..am...... by hospital transport

accompanied by an escort to be nominated by S. N. O. (Admin.).

Escort Cancelled

....
Medical Director
................23 November 1982

Escort returned to Broadmoor at.............................

A 173a

The hospital's form that cancelled the ear scan.

Why would I speak to the guards about trying to escape during the visit? Can you believe the shit they make up? If this was a prison I'd have more rights than this. But the hospital trip was cancelled and I was left to suffer in agony. After that I remember only this: One evening I heard a bang in my head. It was so loud it had actually woken me up. I woke to find blood and pus all over the pillow. Something had burst in my ear. Well, they soon moved their fat arses after that, didn't they? A surgeon was rushed over immediately. He told me I was a very, very lucky man as I had been sleeping on my bad ear. 'Cos if it had burst while I was sleeping on the good ear, the poison would have flowed into my head. It turns out I had a giant abscess behind the left mastoid bone, and it had eventually burst of its own accord.

My life was crazy at times on Norfolk Block but I had some good neighbours. George Shipley and good old Michael Martin. And not forgetting my old china, George Heath. George was a five-foot two-inch fearless powerhouse, a south Londoner who had done a lot of bird in the Scrubs and Parkhurst. He stabbed a grass in jail and was sent here. They said he was a psychopath (like fuck he was). George was just George. If you didn't fuck with him, he wouldn't fuck with you. It was thanks to George that I got to meet Lord Avebury, who was so good in trying to help me.

There was also big Malcolm Morgan. He had spent twenty years in seclusion. I mean twenty years alone, without even a book to read. There was Dickie Langrell, Joe Mercer, Spencer Thorne, Barry Quigley, Dave Wright, Joe Ryan, big John Silver, Dennis Nash, Lenny Doyle, all of them legends in their own right.

Speaking of Dickie Langrell, I remember one time he jumped on my back. He was well into his fifties and only a short geezer, about five foot four inches in height and nine stone dripping wet. He was, I have to say, completely psychotic. He heard voices, and unfortunately one day the voices told him to attack me. Just my luck. He leapt on my back and tried to bite my neck out. I smashed him up into a wall and managed to prise him off (fuck me, he clung like a limpet). The nurses dragged him off, injected him and put him in segregation. I saw him days later, walking around like fuck-all had happened. Madness at its best.

Then there was Chris Reed, Sam Ellis, Ron Greedy, Alan Reeve, so many good men. One loon I remember was just called Malteser Man. He used to have a crap in his pot and then he'd roll little shit balls up, like Maltesers, and ping them across the floor. Totally lunacy. The thing about living in a block like Norfolk is you never know who is going to kick off next. Whose turn is it to have a bad day? Who's going to have a falling-down moment? One day it was Psychotic George's turn. He simply took a pair of scissors and plunged them into another patient several times. When I later asked him why he did it, he said, 'I was fed up, I needed to brighten up the day.'

When something like that did happen, the whole asylum would be on red alert. Bells would immediately go off, whistles would blow, you'd hear a stampede of guards (angels in boots with no wings), with giant syringes ready to pierce your botty. This was living on a razor's edge. One day, one of the Broadmites had a bad day, so he went out onto the yard. He found a fragment of glass, sliced his ball bag open and removed a testicle, which he slung over a wall, along with an attached tangle of gore. Now that is insane. How can a man do that? Think about it for a moment. How? Why? I can close my eyes and still hear the screams, thirty years later. The guards carried him inside, soaked in blood, and injected him while they stitched him up. He was left to sleep in his own nightmare.

Another Broadmite slit his own throat with some glass. So many attempted suicide. Mind you, I don't think that's what The Kite Man had in mind when he jumped twenty feet from the wall. He thought he was a human kite, he really believed that he could fly. Well, until he took the twenty-feet drop and broke both his ankles. He didn't try it again. Norfolk was really living up to its reputation as a hellhole. I spent a good eighteen months on there before Kent Block was mentioned to me. They told me it was more modern than Gloucester Ward and they thought it would be ideal for me. I wasn't so sure myself. Would you be? Broadmoor is Broadmoor, whatever fucking block you're on. Oh well… one must give it a fair go. Let's go!

CHAPTER 4

KENT BLOCK (WARD 3)

'If animals could speak,
would you still eat them?'

Here we fucking go again. Why do I do it to myself? Is there no end to this madness? But don't you just love it? You just never know what's coming next, do you? This is no *One Flew Over the Cuckoo's Nest* fucking shit; this is real-life insanity at its best. I am escorted over to Kent Ward from Norfolk Ward by six guards, all telling me, 'You'll be okay on Kent House. It's very relaxed.' Yeah yeah yeah, where have I heard that before?

My doctor on the new ward is Dr Hamilton, a little Scottish git. I think we had a personality clash from day one. Most psychiatrists are difficult to get on with in my experience, 'cos they seem to know everything, or at least they think they do. And they don't. How can they? They tell me things about me that even I don't know. They need a head shrink themselves. If you work on a farm you smell of shit. If you work in an asylum you smell of madness. Madness has to rub off on you. Mind you, Dr Hamilton did drop my drugs dosage. But that's all he did. Still, anything's gotta be better than Loucas.

Dr Hamilton looks at me perplexed. 'Now, where do we put you? We don't have a spare room so you'll be going into one of the dormitories. There's only twelve of you in there.' Not this shit again. 'That's eleven too many for my liking.' He gave me assurances: 'I promise you now, the first spare room that becomes available will have your name on it.' However, you learn never to trust these fuckers. 'Yeah, and I bet you told the other eleven that one too.'

However, Kent Block actually was more modern. It was also cleaner and lighter, with a more airy feeling about it. The gallery windows looked out to the asylum terrace and it was a wonderful sight. Gardens, flowers, trees, massive oak trees forty feet high, if not higher. There was a bowling green, a summer pavilion, orchards and greenhouses. It was a beautiful view, just like a park. I could see the total freedom. Fuck, I could almost smell it. Oh, and so many types of birds. My favourite is the magpie. Which reminds me, I want to tell you about the most fascinating sight I ever saw in my five years in Broadmoor...

There was a chap here called Peter who was from Essex House. He was in his early fifties and a Trustee as he had been here a good thirty years. Peter was a pleasant chap, always friendly. One day I was looking out of the window, soaking up the glorious day, when I witnessed something I shall never ever forget till the day I die. A magnificent magpie, fully grown with its big white chest, flew down from a tree and landed on Peter's left shoulder. I couldn't believe what I'd just seen. I felt elated. 'Fucking brilliant,' I shouted out to him. Peter looked up and waved at me. I was gob-smacked. It made me feel so fucking good.

I later learnt the backstory to this. That bird had fallen out of its nest as a baby and Peter had taken it back to his cell, feeding it and milking it until it was healthy again. He nursed it until it was well enough for him to release and the bird never forgot it. Most days it would fly down, only to Peter though. Yeah yeah, I know what you're thinking. Total bollocks. Well, you can think what you like; I know what I saw. And every Broadmite from the 1970s and 1980s will know about this, and that it is a fact, so take it or leave it. No way would I have believed it had I not seen it with my own eyes.

I had by now been in Broadmoor for two years and in that space of time I had seen a lot of the old boys die. Legends too. Broadmoor legends. Eric Davies, Alan Deprez, and the oldest old rascal, Walter Prince. Walter had been in the condemned cell in Wandsworth and was waiting to hang. They were gonna stretch his neck. He got reprieved, sectioned and sent here to die. I asked him the big question, 'Would you have rather swung?' He said, 'As far as I am concerned, I died the day I was sentenced to death.'

Walter had killed 22-year-old Harriet Shaw in May 1934, claiming she had given him a venereal disease. He was sentenced to death and then confessed to the murder of George Armstrong, for which a chap called George Fratson was convicted. Prince was considered insane and sent to Broadmoor (Nash, 1993). These were all Broadmites who'd served forty years plus. Walter had been in over fifty years and was almost ninety years old.

I also encountered Eric and Alan. Both diamonds. Both were lovely old boys full of unbelievable stories. Did you know that some of the old folks had arrived at Broadmoor wrapped up in straitjackets on the back of horse-drawn carts? Loads of them had escaped the noose, so they really didn't care if they lived or died. Some of them used to joke about Block 8. 'It' won't be too long. I'll stick around and scare the shit out of the guards,' they'd say with a toothless smile.

Most of the old boys had no teeth: they'd spent fifty years eating sweets and chocolates and neglected brushing their teeth. In fact, in the early days they weren't even allowed toothbrushes, so their teeth gradually rotted and fell out. They all ended up gummy fuckers. But to me, it gave them character.

Kent Block had an ornate conservatory, like a glass extension and a lot of the oldies used to sit in there and play old-time music, like Glenn Miller and the big band numbers. It was really quite an experience and a privilege to share their stories. They all loved Frank Mitchell 'cos he had done the impossible and escaped. Frank was a loveable rogue (well to the loons at least; the guards fucking hated him). He once picked up a whole snooker table. It was like the big Red Indian in *One Flew Over the Cuckoo's Nest*. That's the sort of power he had, an insane amount of strength.

Anyway, enough of the old farts. Let's get back to our new lodgings in Kent. The new dormitory. I suppose I had best start from the beginning. Here we go, strap yourselves in!

My bed was third down from the left wall and I had a window above my headboard, so a nice breeze came in. It felt nice. The guy to my left had come here for strangling a female nurse in a local mental care ward. (Thank fuck I wasn't a female nurse, eh?) He was only small and had these piggy little eyes. He looked like a right shifty little fucker. To my right was Gordon Robinson, a black loon from south London. We never got on from day one. We exchanged words and left it at that, but the atmosphere was icy to say the least. There were always lots of glares between us. Not a great start to dormitory life, is it?!

The others were just your everyday run-of-the-mill loons. Funny fuckers. There was one who would jump up on his bed and have a wank in front of everyone, shouting, 'Look at this for a cock' as he did it. 'Come on mate, put it away. You'll pull it off the way you're going!' someone would shout at him. Even the night guard used to bang on the door. 'Oi, stop that and get into bed before I put you in the seclusion room.' The snores were the same, the snores and the farts and the late-night screams.

Finally the inevitable happened between me and Robinson in the recess. More words were exchanged and it got a bit silly, so I hit him half a dozen times. That was the start of it and it sure wasn't going to end there. We were both our own worst enemies really. Shortly after this incident I am on a visit with Mum and Dad. Visitors were allowed to bring in clothes, food, all sorts (and I don't mean the Bertie Bassett variety). It all goes into a sealed box that is sent over to your block. As I came off my visit I collected my box after the guards had checked it. Fruit, chocolates, some toiletries and a new shirt. I headed to my locker to stash it away when I see Robinson trying a key in my locker. I immediately dropped the box and smashed the granny out of him. I dragged him into the recess and told him, 'If you don't move out of the dorm NOW I will kill you. You will FUCKING DIE IN THAT BED.' And I meant it. I'm not a killer, and I don't ever wish to become one, but at this time I am thinking that if I don't take this cunt out he could do me in my sleep. He had to go. Enough was enough.

If I learned one thing in my short time at Broadmoor it was this: don't ever trust a loon. It's like a rabid dog. Turn your back on it or take your eye off it, it will rip your throat out the first chance it gets. And I am too young to die. Before I go any further, please don't get this incident mixed up with the time I strangled John White in Rampton asylum. White was a child sex killer and I strangled him in the day room. He was clinically dead but the guards resuscitated him. Yes, the guards saved a nonce. Let's hope he was never released to destroy more innocent lives, eh, or it will be on those guards' heads.

Now I don't mention this because I am proud of it. I simply don't want people to mix the two events up. I am stating the facts. I don't wish to be the Boston Strangler here. I don't get a buzz out of strangling anybody, but this cunt Robinson had to go. Steal from me and take the consequences. It was time to take my leave. It was time to turn into mad killer mode. This is what years of Broadmoor madness and maltreatment had driven me to. I felt I had nothing to lose. In my wildest dreams I never ever dreamed I could be so cold and lethal as to contemplate killing a fellow human being, whatever they had done. But it's how it was at the time for me. What choice did I have? This cunt was one problem that was not going to go away. If he'd had half a brain he would have run into the office and demanded to be moved out of the dormitory. Was he also plotting his revenge attack on me? Who knew? In Broadmoor this is what drives us Broadmites on. What's a corpse here or there? One less to feed.

Now, the mauve tie. It was pure silk and my dad had given it to me as a gift (only because I had gone on and on at him about it. He gave in eventually and let me have it). It was the best tie I ever wore. I loved that tie. It was me. My dad's. Special, very special. 'I'm gonna kill this motherfucker with the best tie in the world!'

At 9pm us dormitory loons had to get into our pyjamas and line up to be searched before we were allowed into the dorm. I had the silk tie around my waist, under my pyjamas, and I was first in. I jumped into bed and clocked the rest coming in. In came Robinson. The locker thief. Fucking rat. He glared at me with his one good eye (the other one was swollen and closed). I smiled at him, thinking to myself, 'You daft cunt. You must think I'm an idiot, or else you're very brave or a madman. Whatever.' At 10pm the night watchman shouted, 'Lights off!' and he flicked on the red night light. I knew I had to give it a spell, let all the loons drift off to sleep and into their own nightmares. A few snores started up. The wanker started pounding away as usual. (Fuck me, did he ever get tired?!) At 11pm the guard looked in again.

Once he had left it was time. I knew it was time. I don't really know how I felt. A bit excited, a little unsure perhaps. A bit sad, sad that I was going to throw it all away over a cunt like him. But it was this or I could never relax again. It really was him or me. I know it sounds wicked, and it probably makes me look like a proper nasty git. But I really could see no other way out of it. Just as I lay there, my head willing my body to move, something very weird happened. I believe it was fate. Robinson suddenly moved, then sat up and turned his back to me. He was bending down to put his slippers on. He was obviously going to the toilet. I dived out of the bed and wrapped the tie around his ugly neck and began to choke the bastard. I wasn't expecting the noise he made. It sounded like a horse stuck in a wire. He was gurgling, retching and thrashing about in a panic. It woke the whole dormitory up. Well, all hell broke loose. Loons started shouting and screaming, the guards came tearing in. Robinson was starting to rattle. I kept hold, pulling as tightly as I could. Then something even crazier happened. The tie snapped. I was left with half a tie in each hand. He started to make this terrible noise and his eyes were popping. I noticed then that his face had turned grey. Froth was trickling down his chin and he had shit and pissed himself. I knew immediately I had fast tracked myself back to Norfolk Block. I could see the big welt around his neck. There's no way that tie was 100 per cent silk. How the fuck could it have snapped?

I now believe it was an act of God. Not that I am religious, but I believe it was fate. I was never meant to kill anybody, and I am glad it did snap. It taught me one big lesson: Don't be judge, jury and executioner. But were Broadmoor officials not partly to blame for this? For one thing they KNEW we both had an issue with each other. They could see the facial damage he had, so they would have known something had occurred. Why keep us in the same dorm? They knew all this and still put us together. They also knew how unsettled I had become being in a dormitory. The Rampton incident alone should have served as a warning to the staff at Broadmoor. Don't forget, at this time I was a very unpredictable and violent man. I wasn't myself. I am not, nor ever would, make excuses for my own behaviour. I take full responsibility for my own actions. But why tempt fate? Could it be said that they were neglectful in their duties or their duty of care to Robinson? Perhaps they hoped he would take ME out.

Well, I've left the best bit till last. As it turned out, he had a tool in his pyjama jacket pocket. A blade, which was discovered by the guards as they tried to resuscitate him. They didn't search him too well, did they, when we were all lined up? So he was out to cut me (unless he was planning to do some midnight wood-working!). If I had gone to sleep before him that night I could have well ended up in Block 8. Or survived and ended up with a face like St Pancras Station, full of lines. So all in all, I feel I was right to strike first. My dad was always right! Anyway, as the screws (sorry, 'nurses') all burst in, I pretended I was trying to help him. 'I think he's choking!' I shouted, squeezing his neck. I don't know why but they didn't believe me and I was dragged off to Norfolk.

Now, before we move back to the dreaded Norfolk Block, shall I give you some Kent stories to cheer you all up? Come on, let's take a trip down memory lane, I've got some crackers that you are not going to believe. It was while in Kent that I challenged a loon who was a chess Grand Master. Well fuck me, I won two out of three games, so I became an instant Grand Master. This loon was in Broadmoor for

BROADMOOR HOSPITAL SERIAL A: № 203

INCIDENT / CASUALTY REPORT

Date of Incident / ~~Casualty~~ 16 June 80   Time of Incident / ~~Casualty~~ 1·58 pm   Location NEW WING DORM KENT II

Name(s) of Patient(s)	Hosp. No	House	Ward	RMO
PETERSON M	7347	KENT	III II	

Description of Events leading to Incident/Casualty — EMERGENCY BELL SOUNDED WARD III DORM

Description of Incident/Casualty and extent of any Restraint used — PATIENT CLAIMED THAT PATIENT PETERSON, M WAS TRYING TO STRANGLE HIM. THIS OF COURSE WAS DENIED, NO VISUAL SIGNS OF INJURY APPARENT AND NO RESTRAINT WAS REQUIRED

Witnesses to Incident	Discipline	INDIVIDUAL REPORT ATTACHED YES/NO	Signatures of Witnesses
BENNETT S	S/N		S. Be...
CARROLL S	SEN		
PAYNE R	SEN		
BROWN A	SEN		

Injuries sustained by Staff Patients — NONE

Damage caused to Property : NONE

How was Incident Resolved : EXTRA STAFF SUMMONED, PATIENTS INTERVIEWED

Signature : MO Attending _____   RMO _____

Senior Staff on Duty : D NOEGATE

Incident Report Form concerning the strangling incident.

chopping off the head of someone that had beat him. I had to watch my back with him after that!

Another loon invited me into his cell one evening on association. He said he wanted a cup of coffee and a chat. I thought to myself 'Why not? No harm in it, relieves the boredom.' I tapped on his door and walked in only to find him dressed up in a fucking lacy bra and panties, with a wig on and a face full of make-up. Fuck me, I just burst out laughing. I walked out and shouted out to the loons, 'Come and have a look at this, lads. Quick boys, come and have a butchers!' Even the guards had a laugh at him.

One of the loons on Kent got caught with a blow-up doll… of a sheep! Yes alright, he was Welsh, but it still blew me away. Where the fuck he got it from is beyond me. No doubt it was smuggled in by one of the guards for money. One day some cunt put the Broadmite cat in the spin dryer (I promised not to do it again). Ha ha, okay, I'm joking! But there was fun every day. Such as the day I attended the asylum disco (well, even nuts like to dance). Besides, the girl loons were going, so I decided to stick my name down. Why not? (In hindsight, I wish I hadn't 'cos it was insane. What else did I expect, really?)

I don't really want to bring this name up, but I had best get it out of the way. Jimmy Savile ran the entertainments. He was a Broadmoor official and before you ask me, NO, I never see him doing anything naughty. He was okay with us loons from what I saw. He even once gave me one of his cigars. I handed it out to someone on a visit. Jim was okay from what I saw, but if I knew then what we all know now I would have taken the cunt hostage.

Anyway, moving on. There I was in the visits' room that had been turned into a makeshift disco, lights flashing, great records playing and then the birds came shuffling in, about twenty of them in total. Here comes the totty. Well, some looked like dockers. Lots had

Above left: Mugshot on my entry into Broadmoor, December 1979.

Above right: As the drugs take their toll.

Right: *Maximum Security*: 'My art has been my saviour and I will continue to create.' All works shown here are in some way connected to my time in Broadmoor.

Above: 'Made it, Ma! Top of the world!' Broadmoor's roof tiles have taken a bit of a pasting, though.

Below: *On the Roof* – not every inmate shared my jubilation.

Above: 'Victory is mine!' – just taking a break.

Left: 'I started getting visions of falling off the roof and tumbling down into Block 8,' the Broadmoor cemetery.

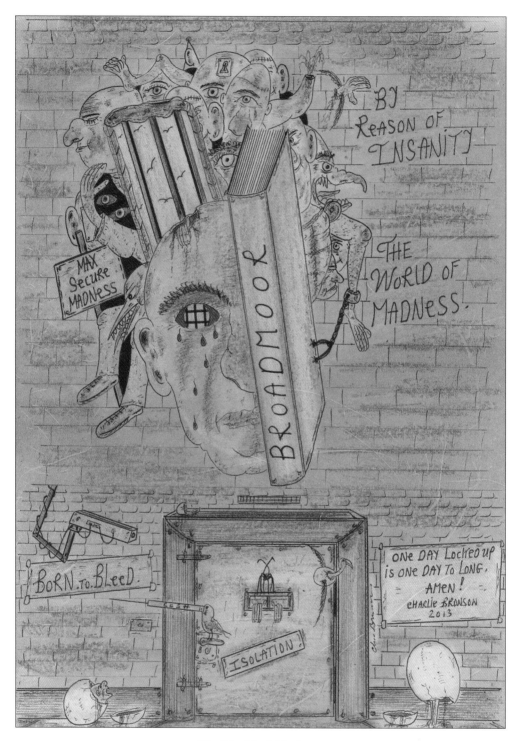

The World of Madness.

Above: *Broadmoor Control Bubble.*

Left: *Liquid Cosh* – as Largactil is colloquially known among inmates 'for its ability to knock out patients, like a cosh over the head'.

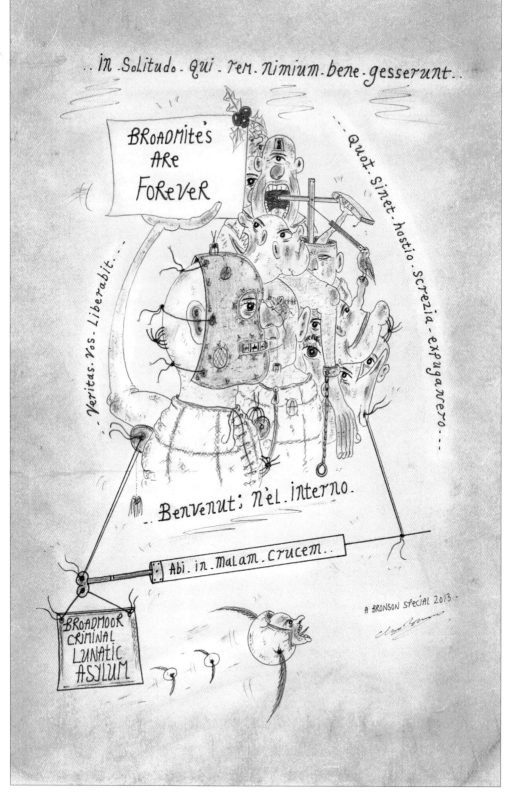

Broadmites Are Forever.

Left: I survived Broadmoor. Could you?

Right: To Survive Broadmoor You Have To Be Special.

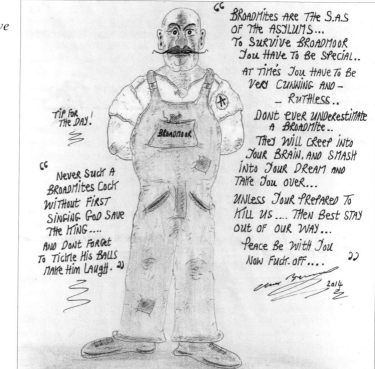

'Gotcha!' – with my soul mate and saviour,
Lorraine, in December 2013.

tattoos and some plainly looked what they were: raving loonies. I watched proceedings from my table. I felt it was the safest place. One girl got overexcited and began kicking her legs high up into the air like a Tiller Girl. She soon got carted off.

One came over to sit at my table. She looked okay, black hair, slim build. Not what I would call pretty, but attractive. 'Hi,' she said. 'Hi,' I said. 'What's your name?' I asked. 'Suzy,' she replied. 'Oh nice, and what are you doing here in the asylum?' When she told me I froze. I felt sickened and my chest felt heavy. 'What? Did she really just say that? Am I dreaming? Is this happening?' I should have known better why she was there. DON'T ask that of anyone sitting in an asylum. Best not to know. She had put her six-month-old baby in the oven with the Sunday roast. This horrible, sick, twisted, evil, stinking baby killer. I hated her. 'Fuck off. Go on, get the fuck away from my table, you horrible cunt.' I wanted to spit in her face but held back. 'Go on, fuck off.' She disappeared out of sight. The guards were all stood around the room, watching every move. One came over to me and asked if everything was alright. I said, 'Yeah, why shouldn't it be?'

Then my favourite record came on. Procol Harum's 'A Whiter Shade of Pale'. I love it, it's a good slow one, a good smoochy dance. I was approached by a big black bird. She had a gorgeous face, but a big body. She looked strong, with a lot of muscle tone. 'Do you want to dance?' she said. 'Who me? Yeah, it's my favourite song.' So off we went into the middle of the floor and held on for a slow one. Fuck me, it was good. She smelt nice too. I've got to say now, it really did feel nice. You wouldn't get this in Parkhurst or Dartmoor. If only the lads could see me now. But then she started to get silly. She was taller than me, and probably three stone heavier. A big girl, around thirty-five years old. She started to squeeze my neck with her forearm, tighter and tighter. It was fucking crazy… and very embarrassing. I didn't wish to nut her but I had to put a stop to this and fast, before I was too dizzy to stop it. This could end up with me in Block 8, and all for a fucking dance! 'Lunatic bird strangles Charlie Bronson on the dance floor.' No man wants that for an ending.

Anyway, I managed to untangle myself and fuck her off. Now I am very angry. I feel like I'm gonna blow up and lose it, so I decided to take my leave early. I walked to the door and asked the guard to get me back to Kent Block quick as you like. 'I've had enough, I'm bored of this shit.'

Kent Block wasn't without its problems. One big fat paedo got a tool shoved in his ear in the toilet, down by the playing fields. He ended up a vegetable. No one got nicked for it. Justice at its best, I say. Another slipped down a flight of stairs and fractured his skull. Some said the fracture happened before he fell. Again, no one was around when it happened. Another had cooking oil tipped over his head while he was sat on the crapper having a shit. Lots of crazy things were happening, so I was actually glad when I was dragged back to Norfolk.

This time I knew it was for good. I knew it and they knew it. And guess what? I really did not care. Us Broadmites don't lose sleep over spilt milk. We sleep with a smile and awake prepared. Today could be a lucky day. Could you live our existence? Being controlled 24/7. Pumped up with psychotropic tranquillisers, never knowing when or if you will ever walk free. Go and visit the polar bears in the zoo, do they look happy? Look at their heads going up and down, clock their body movements. Those bears are depressed; they're being driven insane. I bet you all I've got that their food is drugged up to keep them docile. Tigers and lions are the same, and so are us humans. Broadmoor was driving us mad, the cause of all of our problems.

But now it was nearing the time for me to give these people the biggest problem their asylum had ever experienced. Nobody on this planet fucks with me as you have done. Even the half-decent guards now had a problem with me. They knew trouble was coming and they knew why. But they didn't know when or how it would erupt. They were like chickens without heads, clucking like constipated cockerels. Norfolk Block opened up and sucked me back in, with a big smile. I had a vision, a picture in my head. I knew what my next move was going to be. I just needed to be cool and patient, sit back with a smile on my face and bide my time. I am going to fuck Broadmoor and I am prepared to die to do it. My next move after this could well be to Block 8. But whatever happens, I am truly ready. They have created me. I am only what they have made me into, a desperate man in need of some serious payback. Let's do this!

CHAPTER 5

NORFOLK
BLOCK

'Never walk backwards into a madman's nightmare.
Believe me, you won't get back out.'

'Welcome back. Behave or you're gonna get the shit kicked out of you.' BANG. The door slams shut and I'm back in my own seclusion pad. A mattress, a jug of water and a piss-pot. But I feel strangely alive. Prepared. It's now a waiting game for me. A bit like planning a job. It's actually quite exciting. A happy feeling, one of elation.

You're actually one up on them because you know something they don't. If they find out then you're fucked, but how can they find out if you don't tell anyone? Unless you talk in your sleep. In which case, sew your lips up. This is the big one, so don't fuck it up. Hey, while the cat's away the mice did play. These cunts had been very naughty to the Broadmites, nicking the best food, bashing them up, drugging them, basically causing a lot of unnecessary shit as usual. Fucking bully boys.

I pulled a couple of them and told them to have a word with their firm and pack it in. Days later I was being escorted off the yard to my cell when they jumped me. No reason whatsoever, it was totally out of the blue and they were mob handed, the only way they could ever work. Some were punching and kicking me, although a couple weren't really wanting to be involved. One shouted 'Enough!' I was slung in my cell and the door slammed shut. All fucking day I kicked that door and shouted pure abuse. They never unlocked my door for days, just shoved food and water through the hatch in the wall. In prison they would never have got away with this shit (and that's saying something). I used to watch the loonies through my hatch and sometimes they would peer in on me. I'd see them looking in, their eyes spaced out, mouths open. Some would have a sick, lost look, standing there dribbling. I'd tap the hatch and shout, 'You okay? You alright?' Some would nod, but some would just stand there, silent and motionless until a guard spotted them. 'Oi, get the fuck away from that hatch!'

It was around this period I found out why the custard was so sweet. They were putting Largactil in it (see the Drugs Index, page 195). It was making me so unwell, drowsy and lethargic. I knew it was the custard. Every time I ate it I felt unwell. I was getting fed up of all these games. These bastards were nicking the canteen out of our boxes. I loved it when I found out about the character we called 'The Sweet Man'. He would always have a bag of sweets on him, carrying them around and offering them to the screws. He never offered any to his fellow patients and one day I pulled him over this. 'Oi, why you giving sweets to them slags and not your mates?' I said. He said, 'Because I don't like the screws.' Eh? That made no sense. It was then that he told me he used to stick half a dozen up his arse of a night, and return them to their packet in the morning. He'd been doing it for years. What a great guy. They deserved it too, the slags. Stealing our own food that we paid for.

They were also fucking with our mail. They were just out to wind us up with silly little games, day in and day out. Kicking our doors and flicking our lights on and off in the early hours. Sometimes we would go out on the yard and come back to find a jug of water had mysteriously spilt onto our mattress. The showers were always cold, purposely. It seemed to be every little thing, and the little things that people take for granted. Razors were completely blunt so you cut yourself to ribbons, soap we got was already covered in hairs. I'd even seen scouring powder (like the old Vim you used to get) put in patients' tea and cocoa. A slipper would disappear (what fucking use is one slipper? If you didn't look like a lunatic before, you would now, walking around with one slipper on). To add to all this bollocks, we had virtually fuck-all in our cells… sorry, rooms… we should call them 'rooms' as we are, of course, in a 'hospital'. (Still think Broadmoor is a hospital, readers?) We weren't allowed any books, newspapers or magazines, nothing. No pens, pencils, radios, music. Nothing. We were being denied all forms of human rights, which even prisoners were allowed. It was a total piss-take.

One day the guards came into my cell with some clothes. 'Get ready, you're on a visit,' they bellowed. I wasn't given any notice and I had no idea who it was I was meant to be seeing. I was going through a bad time at this stage and had cut off visits from everyone: family, friends, everyone. When I'm going through bad times I often cut off. I could have asked them who it was I was meant to be visiting, but I wasn't talking. I was so tensed up and angry. They marched me to the visits room and it was only Terry Downes and Mickey Zanes.

Nicknamed the 'Paddington Express', Terry Downes won the World Middleweight Title on 11 July 1961, defeating Paul Pender at

Wembley, England, and he once held the Middleweight Champion Belt of the World. A proper loved and respected cockney, he grabbed my hand and whispered, 'Ronnie Kray's concerned about you, so we've come to see you're okay. What do you need?' I was overwhelmed. 'Fuck me Terry, I'm okay. Don't you guys worry about me,' I said. A guard clocked this and marched over. A big fat twat I didn't like. He said to Terry, 'Wasn't you the British Champion?' Terry winked at me and smiled then said to the fat twat, 'The world, Sonny. Get it right. The world.' It didn't stop him asking for a signed photo. Terry said, 'On your way mate, I'm talking to my pal here.' It was a priceless moment, to see one of the nasty fuckers taken down a peg or two. He made him look a right prick. Perhaps for a moment he knew how it felt to be made to feel like you're less than human, like they made us loons feel 24/7.

Terry signed some photos for me and my family and Mickey stuck a ton in my canteen spends. We had a great visit and it did wonders to lift my spirits. I shook his hand and whispered, 'Tell Ronnie I've got something I'm putting together. You'll see it on the news very, very soon Terry.' He smiled and said, 'Be safe.'

That visit propelled me into some serious training. I was starting to feel powerful again. I laughed a lot, sang a lot. I began to feel like I was on fire, a man on a mission. The guards had even started to chill out a bit with us. Even the other Broadmites had noticed how much easier it was. The tension seemed to be receding. I would start singing a good old number at night-times, something like 'San Quentin' or 'Tie a Yellow Ribbon' or a good old Christmas carol. Half of the loons always joined in with me, it was like a Broadmoor choir. Fucking brilliant. But my ultimate favourite was 'When the Saints Go Marching In'. You can get a good old kick out of that song.

It was good times for us; it felt like there was some solidarity. I loved the guys. Why wouldn't I? We were all in this together. Sadly some were too far gone and they just slept. They probably never even heard us they were so dead to the world. But we were alive and kicking. Party time!

It must have been around this time that I first met Lord Avebury and struck up a friendship with him when he came to Broadmoor. In fact, he came to visit my old buddy, George Heath. George was fighting his being sent to Broadmoor, and rightly so. He was 100 per cent jailbird, a true convict with massive principles. He hated Broadmoor and made it clear to everyone that he would actually kill someone and return to prison rather than spend his time with the loonies, and he meant every word of it. And George wasn't too fussy about who he wasted either! Anyway, I managed to have a few words with Lord Avebury this particular day.

If I may say so, I felt he was worthy of being a Broadmite himself. He was quite mad and very eccentric; I really warmed to him. He was into Buddhism and spoke to me about his views on death. I won't tell you what he told me because it's personal, but it was very eerie.

I was in contact with him for a couple of years, via mail, and he tried his best to improve certain aspects of our lives in Broadmoor but an institution like this is so deeply embedded in its Victorian ways, and run by such power freaks, that they are a law unto themselves. I have to send my respects to Lord Avebury, even though I've not had any contact with him for over two decades. As Lords go, he was a gentleman and a larger-than-life character, with a hell of a smile. I would go as far as to say he is fearless, because not many would dare try to change such a hellhole, or have the backbone to face us Broadmites, to sit and discuss our issues, and try to help us.

Yeah, I salute the old bugger, Lord Broadmite, a top geezer! But let's face it, there was only one Lord of the Manor: Ronnie Kray.

With his silk ties, crocodile shoes and immaculate suits, Ronnie lived it up there. And he had the pick of the bum holes! It must be bloody fantastic to be homosexual in the asylums. How cruel it is for us heterosexuals, though. What a wicked world.

CHAPTER 6

UP ON THE ROOF:
PART I

(21 MAY 1981)

It was a horrible rainy day on 21 May 1981 when six of us Broadmites were being trusted to be escorted over to the canteen (with ten guards accompanying us, mind you). The big, fat slob of a guard was one of them. He was still embarrassed over being mugged off by Terry Downes and I made sure he never forgot it. I used to say to one of them, 'Did you hear how Terry fucked your mate off?' It really riled him up. I even overheard him say to his colleague, 'Let's dope that prick up. He's getting on my fucking nerves.'

Heh-heh, I was getting right under his skin. Other times I would sing. 'Who ate all the pies?' I hated him. Mind you, he hated me, too, the nasty git, and sadly he had the upper hand to fuck me up. The drugs. A word in the doctor's ear was all it took. Plus 'natural' spillage. That's how it works in Broadmoor. They spill a bit on purpose and it finds its way into places it shouldn't be. So anyway, there we are on our way to the canteen. I had waited weeks, months, for this. This is going to be my big moment. There was no going back now. It's do or die. LET'S FUCKING DO THIS!

BROADMOOR HOSPITAL				SERIAL A: № 2580

INCIDENT / CASUALTY REPORT

Date of Incident / Casualty	21. 5. 81	Time of Incident / Casualty	APPROX 2·20 PM	Location	Between ESSEX + KENT HOUSES.

Name(s) of Patient(s)	Hosp. No.	House	Ward	RMO
PETERSON M.	7347	NORFOLK	3.	DR LUCAS

Description of Events leading to Incident/Casualty
PATIENT HAS RECENTLY BEEN CONCERNED ABOUT HIS RETURN TO PRISON BEING DELAYED ALTHOUGH IN THE LAST WEEK HE HAS SHOWN NO APPARENT ANXIETY AS TO HIS POSITION. IT IS ASSUMED THAT THIS INCIDENT IS A MANOUVER TO DRAW ATTENTION TO HIS PLIGHT.

Description of Incident/Casualty and extent of any Restraint used
WHILST ESCORTING NORFOLK W03 PATIENTS TO CANTEEN, THE ABOVE NAMED PATIENT CLIMBED UP THE STATION, BETWEEN ESSEX + KENT +, ONTO THE ROOF OF KENT HOUSE

ALTHOUGH THE ESCORTING STAFF HAD TAKEN EVERY PRECAUTION AGAINST SUCH AN INCIDENT OCCURING THE PATIENT WAS FAR TO QUICK FOR THEM

Witnesses to Incident	Discipline	INDIVIDUAL REPORT ATTACHED YES/NO	Signatures of Witnesses
RUSSELL	C.N.		
GRIFFITHS.	S.N.	YES.	
PITHER.	S.N.		
BELTON.	S.N.		Pitton.
BOLAND.	S.N.		P. Boland.

Injuries sustained by Staff: NONE
Patients: NONE

Damage caused to Property :

How was Incident Resolved :

Signature : MO Attending .... RMO ....

Senior Staff on Duty : ....

Incident Report Form about the first roof protest.

I break free and start to run. Whistles blow and I hear footsteps charging behind me, size 10 boots pounding after me and shouts of 'Oi, stop.' Like fuck I will. I'm off like a greyhound with its arse on fire. I reach the iron structure and jump, grabbing onto a bar. As I pull myself up someone grabs hold of my right ankle. I kick out with my left foot and look down. It's only the fat twat who gets it in the crust. BANG! He goes down like a sack of spuds.

As I clambered up the drainpipe my knuckles were hitting the wall behind it, but I knew I couldn't afford to let go. I make it up to the roof and swing over to Kent House, grabbing the drainpipe. I'm going up like a rat on a hot wire, but the rain is making it very slippery and I can't hold on properly. But I make it up to the old guttering. It's loose, very loose, and it's wet and I am by now drenched. But I make it up. YEEEE-FUCKING-HAR! I am the king of this castle.

And it was at that moment I clocked it. A beautiful rainbow. The most beautiful rainbow I've ever seen, right above my head. It felt wonderful. Champion! I felt like this was a message, a sign. 'You done well, my son.' What a feat. What a climb. Everest next! Ha. Nothing is impossible. NOTHING!

Within half an hour Dr McGrath, the Superintendent, appeared on the scene, peering from the window on Ward Three. He looked crushed. You see I had to make it this exact week. This had been planned for months and it had to be this exact week I did it. Next week would have been too late. And do you know why? After twenty-four years as boss of Broadmoor, this week was McGrath's retirement week. I crushed him before he left. A mad Broadmite had bought him to his knees. I'd crippled him. Don't get me wrong. I didn't dislike Dr McGrath. But he had to take responsibility for the brutality in his prized refractory block and the whole godforsaken place he ran. You can't tell me he didn't know what was going on. He had to know, the whole asylum knew. It was run on fear, an iron fist, and his staff were fucking bullies. Cowards and bullies and they were under HIS charge, running wild with their drug control and violence. Years of misery, beatings and abuse by the very people who had a duty of care to mentally ill people.

McGrath practically begged me. 'Please don't damage the roof.' I shouted to him, 'Fuck off and get me some cheese rolls, a flask of coffee and a cream cake, then we will talk. And stick some spring onions in the rolls.' I warned him that if he tried to send the heavy mob up on the roof I'd grab one and jump off. 'Now fuck off and get my grub.' He did, and I got it within half an hour. He passed it through the window to me. I grabbed it and found myself a nice spot to have a picnic, sitting down to enjoy my grub.

The sun had by now come out, the showers long gone. I took most of my clothes off and laid them on the slates of the roof to dry. Hell's bells, I felt free. Free and alive, and those cheese rolls were the best I'd ever had. Don't worry, I checked them for drugs… and the cake as well. I'm not silly. Those cunts don't pull one on us Broadmites. Definitely not whilst up on a high roof. I heard my name being called. It was Roger Russell, one of the nurses from Norfolk Block. He was now at the window. Roger was always respectful to me, and he had stopped a lot of shit. He asked me what my protest was about and how long it would last. (What it was about? Fuck me, where do I start?!) I just said, 'Tell the Superintendent thanks for the grub and coffee. Now say goodbye to your roof. World War III has arrived.' Broadmoor Lunatic Asylum was about to be crushed.

Those asylum slates back in the 1980s cost a fiver each. Nowadays they are maybe £30 each. And Kent's a massive roof, with a lot of slates. But I was ready and it was time. BANG! For the first ten hours I don't think I stopped. It was fucking magical. Kent Block was quickly evacuated. Fuck knows where they went (who cares?). I skimmed the slates, aiming them at the workshop windows. CRASH, One- hundred and eighty! I even got some over the top of the wall, smashing cars in the car park (I hope I got Loucas's car, the evil swine). Just by the car park is the Broadmoor Guards' Social Club. I even got a few through their windows.

The police, fire brigade and ambulance services were all out there on standby, and then the television cameras turned up. There were hundreds of members of the public gathered, nosey onlookers stopping to watch the show. Some were cheering, or shouting, 'Jump, jump!' Nasty fuckers! Fuck me, I was thirsty. My throat was parched, my eyes were full of shit and dust and my fingers were full of splinters and bleeding. Nails had ripped my back and arms and my body ached. I was near to exhaustion but three quarters of the slates were up.

I then started on the rafters. I tore out electrical wiring, copper piping, I even got through to the ceiling. There were holes everywhere. Before long the light started to fade. Most of the onlookers had started to fade away, returning to their cosy little homes and their loving families. I lay on the roof looking up at the stars. At night-time it was like Hollywood, big beams of light shining up on me, trained on my every move. I was free and happy. Or was I? How could I be? This fucking hellhole was squeezing all my dreams away. I had none left. I had lost everything, even my mind. When a man loses his way he becomes something not very nice. I never liked myself. I think maybe I was battling with who I had become, what this hellhole had made me. It all sounds crazy, but then again it is. How can it be anything else?

Fuck me, it was beautiful up here. I found myself some plastic, a roll of felt and some sacking and made a bed. It was a gorgeous evening so I broke out into song, another of my all-time favourites, 'When

Will I See You Again?' by The Three Degrees. That was number one back in 1974 when I was on remand. I love that song. I loved music, always have and always will. You could say I'm a soul man. I was a Tamla Motown freak, I loved the 1960s and the soul sounds of the '70s. This rapping crap just don't do it for me and never will.

Oh, an owl. I spotted an owl. A FUCKING OWL, hooting away on the Essex roof, and I could see it in all its glory. A real live owl with massive eyes and beautiful head movements. I had heard it many times before from my cell, but I'd never seen it. It was magnificent, a real treat to see. What a beauty. Owls are wise. Smart. A bit like us Broadmites.

I looked up at the night sky. Those stars looked mysterious. Lying there looking up at them it made me think about what life is really all about. What is the purpose of life? Who knows? Who will ever know? At this time in my life the one real strength I had on the outside world was my wonderful sister Loraine. We were always close and in each other's hearts. Some would say too close. But that's how we were, very close. She's so lovely and loving to me. She's always there and the bond we have is almost psychic. I definitely don't deserve her. But I idolise her. She is a massive strength to me in times of badness. I always see her face in my dreams. She's always with me. We laugh a lot, chat a lot. I only have to look in her eyes and I feel a rush of goodness. She's a living, breathing angel. My angel. Not sure what I am to her, maybe a good brother. I do love my Loraine and as I write this today, over thirty years later, we are even closer. So what does that tell you? It tells me one thing: she is the greatest angel to me on this fucked up planet…

I drifted off into my first freedom sleep in years. No locks, no doors. Shut away from all eyes in a little den up on the roof overlooking the Berkshire countryside. Fuck Broadmoor. Fuck the world.

I awoke stiff, wet and very, very cold. My back felt like I had been trampled on by a flock of elephants. A flock of elephants (no hang on, that don't sound right. It's a herd of elephants. Flock is birds). Anyway, flock or herd, I was in a bad way. My breathing was not right. There was a lot of stabbing pain in the kidney area. I really wasn't in a good way. When I coughed, my chest hurt. Looking back now, I think I breathed in lots and lots of asbestos. The entire attic was covered in the poison. I had also caught pleurisy. The damp had soaked into my skin and my body, attacking my organs. I had a scramble round and found the water tank. Floating on top of the water was a dead bat, but I had no choice, I was so thirsty I had to drink it. Then I ate some moss from the gutter and a couple of pigeon eggs. I then spotted a dead pigeon. I sliced it open with a slate and ate it. Within half an hour I was shitting through the eye of a needle. I was badly sick. I made sure I shat through a hole in the ceiling so it splattered into Kent Ward Three.

During my second day on the roof I started getting visions of falling off the roof and tumbling down into Block 8. I was in a bad, bad way. Then it hit me. This smell. One of the most delicious smells you can imagine. The type that makes you salivate even when you're not hungry… and I was fucking starving. Below me they were frying bacon and onions and the smells were wafting up into the loft. The dirty evil fuckers. (Did you know they do that in all prison rooftop protests, to make you hungry and try to remind you you're fucking starving to death?) It's actually a brilliant ploy on their part, a great psychological move.

I blocked my nose up with paper. I was watching all the activity over the wall. There were loads of teenagers jumping up and down, shouting, 'Jump, jump!' I'll put money on it they were the guards' kids. These asylums were made up of generations of guards (great-grandfather, grandfather, father, son); it was a profession where they seemed to follow each other into it, they are born into it. Insanity was their life too. Come on, admit it, it runs in families. Insanity breeds. Believe me some of these guards were as mad as March hares. They can't work sixty, seventy hours a week in a nuthouse and not take it home with them. Could you? There is no escape from Broadmoor, it's in your blood. We ARE Broadmoor. It's our world. It's actually a blessing, it really is. An historic and famous place like this and we are all actually a part of it, a part of that history.

It's like Colditz. If you were there and survived that, then I salute you. The same as survivors of Auschwitz and Bergen-Belsen. You can't but be proud to have survived such atrocities. Even the guards. After a day's work (if you call it work), if they could walk out of the gate after a twelve-hour shift without having been punched, kicked, spat on or having had a pot of shit thrown over their head, it was a good day. They'd survived. Believe me, many did walk out broken men. It's all about survival in my book. And right now, up on this roof, my chances ain't looking so good.

Fuck me, my back's killing me. I can't see me surviving this. I think I actually fell asleep again. By the third day I was in a seriously bad way, and I knew it. I had actually convinced myself it was over for me. But in a strange sense it felt like a lovely way to die. A victorious end. These cunts would never forget me. And it would at least be *my* ending. Then I heard someone shouting, 'You alright up there son?' I looked down and saw my dad and two brothers Mark and John standing alongside the officials. 'You okay, son?' Dad shouted. 'Fuck me Dad, what you doing here?' He called up again. 'Come down boy, you've made your point. Time to come down, son.'

John, my elder brother, was a Royal Marine and Mark was Royal Navy. Both proud but fair men. Dad was ex-Royal Navy. Me? I never did join up. You could say I was my own force. My self-discipline was second to none and my instinct to survive is 100 per cent. Would I have come down that day had it not been for my dad and brothers? Do you know something, I don't think I would have. Come down to what? More madness, more drugs, more brutality. Years of nothing but an empty room. Would a sane man have come down for that? I shouted down, 'Fish and chips, mug of tea …maybe?! Oh and some apple pie and custard. The pink custard. And I want half an hour with you three.'

The officials agreed. They told me to stay where I was and they put a ladder up through Ward 3. I said, 'Fuck off, I'll come down the same way I came up!' They shouted, 'Don't do that, it's too dangerous!' but I am dangerous. 'Watch this!' I shouted. How the fuck I made it down is beyond me. I could barely use my fingers. I really was in a terrible state.

Once I reached the ground, the first person to come over to me was guard Roger Russell. He told me what would happen next. No funny games, no trouble, I was being taken to the medical room to be checked over. The multitude of splinters in my hands were removed and my eyes were washed out to clean them of all the debris. The Medical Officer confirmed I had got pleurisy. I had a hot bath to warm up and I was led to a room where Dad, John and Mark were. We had a good natter, said our goodbyes and I was then taken to my cell where my demands were waiting. I gulped the lot down in record time and them rolled over on the bed, slipping into a dream state.

I slept for England. I think I even had a smile on my face. I have left out one little detail for the end of this story. That slag Dr Loucas came into my cell and said to me, and I quote, 'You will NEVER get another chance to do that. You have just buried yourself.' Fuck off cunt. SLAM. And that was it for me, for a very, very long time. But I always remembered his words. And at that moment, deep in my heart

I felt – and thought – 'You'll be sorry you ever said that to me. *You* will be sorry, cunt.'

The next two years, I have to say, I really don't remember a lot about, which is probably a good thing. My medication was dragging me down. I slept most of my life away. I also went through a serious bout of depressing thoughts. Block 8 was constantly on my mind. I got a morbid sense of doom. I felt like I had failed, let down all my family.

I got Loraine up for a one-to-one chat. I told her how I really was and what I was feeling. I could feel myself slipping away from reality. All my nice dreams had gone. I felt ugly and angry all the time. I think I actually cried on that visit. I told her, 'I'm not having this shit any more. I'm tired of being abused and hearing all the screams of the tortured souls.' She asked me, 'What can I do?' I said, 'I'm not sure, but expect something from me, and soon. I'm not telling another soul, but I'm about to do something that will bring this asylum to its knees. Let's leave it at that. Now, how's the kids? How's Mum? What's going on it Luton, is it nice? Any flowers in the garden?'

We always hold hands. It's wonderful and my Loraine always smells of heaven. A beautiful smell. Eyes that shine. Teeth so perfect. It's like sitting talking to an angel. I'm so blessed. After a visit with Loraine I always felt a surge of inner strength, a buzz of energy. A happy feeling of being wanted and loved. Basically, I was made to feel human. Then it's back to insanity.

You have to be mad to survive this place. All the insane acts around you, the violence, the screams. It all soaks into your brain like a sponge. You are being moulded and manipulated by a wicked, evil system. Around this time, Mum sent me in a yoga book. I had never done any yoga, and luckily the officials decided I could have it in my cell. It became like a Bible to me. I learnt so much from that book.

It kept me in good shape, healthy and ultra-supple. I also got into meditation. I could actually achieve it and it felt so good. It made me feel like I was back in control of my life. Yoga is a fantastic discipline to master.

One night I was lying on my bed, in my own little world and I heard a tapping on the wall. It was my neighbour, John Silver. He called me to the hatch from his hatch. We could speak quietly, whispering to each other. He asked me if I could get him a plastic bag, or a razor. I'm now in shock. He had come to his end and he wanted out. A Block 8 candidate, a dead man mumbling. A terrible blackness came over me as we had this discussion. I felt so sad and angry. Here was a loon wanting to die, and I'm supposed to help him and listen to his pain and suffering.

I will now explain to you the miracle surrounding this incident, and believe me when I tell you it was 100 per cent down to my yoga and meditation. John Silver and me were serious arch enemies. John Erico Silver took his wife and four children on a picnic near Littlehampton, Sussex. He tied his wife up but she escaped, and he then took a hammer to his children, killing all four of them. He pleaded not guilty to murder but guilty to the charge of manslaughter at Chester Assizes on 19 December 1968. He was sectioned under Section 60 of the Mental Health Act 1959 and sent to Broadmoor. Well, I despised the cunt, so much so I wished only badness on him, but it's a long story so I'll start at the beginning.

Back in 1969 Silver was on the remand unit in Brixton Prison at the same time as the Kray's' firm, and he stuck out from everybody. He was six feet ten-and-a-half inches and an ex-Guardsman from Buckingham Palace. With that bearskin hat on he would have been about nine fucking foot tall. A giant. Silver was despised by the cons and screws alike. He had killed his kids with a claw hammer. Four innocent little kiddies. He was eventually found to be insane and sent to Broadmoor.

He became a bit of a Broadmite legend for chinning the guards and once he even chinned a doctor. He obviously had serious issues. I collared him in the recess one day and chinned him. Just for the sake of it, yes, because I despise child killers (plus I wanted the experience of knocking out a giant, it's good for the CV!). It felt good too. But he had spent the last ten years in solitary with fuck-all (and I do mean fuck-all). He had lost so much weight; I believe he went from about nineteen stone down to twelve. He looked haggard, sick, like a cancer victim. His eyes were sunken into his face. It was not a nice sight, from a giant of a man to this. His back was bent, arched and he trembled a lot.

I NEVER spoke to him in the two years of him being next to my cell. All I ever did was verbally abuse him. Until I started the yoga. My breathing got calmer, my mind felt at peace. I just felt different. I can't explain how or why (fuck me, don't worry, I'm not going soft on child killers, don't you worry about that). But when he spoke I just felt 'Fucking hell, how much can one man take? What's left for him?' And if the truth be told, yes, I felt for him. He took some serious beatings, make no bones about it. There didn't seem to be a week that passed where he wasn't involved in a scuffle with the guards, and I know because I heard the beatings, the attacks on him from ten to twelve guards. The boots and punches going in. I heard his screams as the syringe went in. (Don't worry, I also remembered his kids and how they must have screamed. And his wife. In fact, I believe she may have survived.)

I don't know what happened this evening with Silver, but I just changed, inside. I told him, 'Pack it in now. Get a fucking grip of yourself. Block 8 is a very lonely place. You don't want to go there.

Behave yourself and shake your crust. Where there's life, there's hope.' He just listened as I spoke. 'You've gotta dig deep and pull out of this negative shit. It's just a bad spell. It will pass.'

He did work himself through his bad period. Later in 1984 he was transferred to Ashworth asylum and I believe he was freed in the early 1990s. (How fucking ironic is that? A multiple murdering madman is released and I am still stuck in this shitty, hypocritical system.) He's probably out there somewhere today, a very lonely old man, 'cos I don't know how a man can carry that sort of guilt around with him. I did ask him why he did that to his kids. He told me that the world was evil and he loved them and did it to protect them. That was obviously his madness. I hate him for what he did, but I just felt that a little humanity wouldn't go amiss here. The guards would have loved for him to top himself and make his journey to Block 8. It's probably why I helped him that evening. Just to piss the guards off. John Silver will always be a legendary Broadmite in my book, simply for how he came up against the mob-handed bully boys. I wish him no harm or badness in his journey of life, but John, if you are reading this, stay the fuck away from me. I am still confused as to how or why I helped such a monster, but strangely it made me feel human. (See, proves I'm not all bad, I do have feelings. Let's just leave it at that, things like that ruin my street cred.)

Life rolled on and 1983 felt like it was going to be a lucky year for me. I had now gotten into poetry and I loved it. I wrote one called 'Block 8'. I even got a small poetry book called *LIFE* produced. Me, a poet, an author and a yogi. It was all looking bright for me. But I still had something to put right. Unfinished business, and like the proverbial elephant, I never forget. And it was soon to be my time for revenge. I had decided I was going to have a night on the tiles. Why not? (Could I? How?) Nothing's impossible for a Broadmite. Before we get to that exciting episode, shall we have a poem? You probably think 'Him, a poet? No way, he's a loon. It's all in his head. Poetry my arse!' Well, I am a poet, and a proud one at that. And here's the proof.

Block 8, by Himself (The Broadmite Poet) 1983

Everyone speaks of Block 8
It feels very creepy
Old Loonies fear it
They become very weepy
So many end up there
Long before their time
Insanity is very dark
Broadmoor is a crime

Block 8 is in the shadows
Broadmites forever asleep
 There is no escape from madness
Start to count the sheep
In and out of dreams
Nightmares come and go
Fading into loneliness
Covered in freezing snow

Fuck you Block 8
You're never ever taking me
Mad men without faces
This madman will walk free
The key to life is precious
Blood pours from my heart

Broadmites fly to heaven
I knew it from the start

I kiss the apple pie
It makes me feel so good
Us Broadmites love the world
I hope it's understood
We march on together
Through the madness, thick and thin
We have nothing to lose, everything to win

Fuck you Block 8
You're not taking us
It's over the wall for Xmas
We will catch the bus
I'm the poet from Hell
Born again for sure
I create my feelings
All behind this door.

I dedicated this poem to Ruth Ellis. Ruth Ellis was the last woman to be hanged in the UK, after being convicted of the murder of her lover David Blakely. On Easter Sunday 1955, Ellis shot Blakely dead outside the Magdala public house in Hampstead, north London. She immediately turned herself over to the police and at the resulting trial, took full responsibility for the murder. She was hanged at Holloway Prison on 13 July 1955 by the famous executioner (or infamous, as you may view it) Albert Pierrepoint. Murdered by an evil state. In France it would have been deemed a crime of passion and she'd have been freed. But we stretched her neck. A beautiful lady. Her sister used to do my mother's hair. Ruth was lovely, a beautiful lady. RIP Ruth.

Oh well, one mustn't rabbit on, I've a roof to pull off. Oh but before I do, as we're talking about hanging, I want to ask you a question. Would you prefer to hang – or see out your days in Broadmoor? Come on, which would you choose? Have a think about it and get back to me (or perhaps you should wait until we get to the end of my journey here, then you can make a more informed decision). The noose awaits, the trap door is being oiled or you can ride off towards the gates of Hell into Broadmoor, and become a celebrated Broadmite, officially a lunatic and the world will never look at you in the same way again – if you ever make it back out, that is.

CHAPTER 7

UP ON THE ROOF: PART II, DAY 1

(19 JUNE 1983)

'Made it, Ma! Top of the world!'
James Cagney as Cody Jarrett in *White Heat* (1949)

I did have my doubts this time around. It really was a bastard of a climb, and it had to be done with precision timing. It was a bit like an SAS operation, get in fast and you can't afford any fuck-ups. Two years seemed like a long enough wait, I was now ready mentally and physically for my encore. It was either do it now or keep dreaming, and I had to do it today because it was a lovely sunny day. My only concern was what yard I was going to be on. It had to be the big yard. The smaller yard would destroy all of my plans. By now I was getting excited at the prospect of repeating my feat. When the guard said, 'Let's use the big yard today, it's lovely and sunny', I almost cheered out loud. Holy fucking shit, it's on. It's here. Let's do it.

I shuffled out with my 'Fuck me, I'm bored' face', all the time clocking the guards' postures and stance. They were all stood in their usual positions to observe us. Young George Shipley was with me and I'd confided to him what my plan was. He wanted to do it with me but bless him, George was on a lot of medication and I knew he would never make it. This climb was a suicide mission and I didn't want his death on my conscience.

There is a brick-house toilet on this yard, approximately seven feet in height, maybe eight. My plan was to leap up and from there, dive about six feet across onto a window bar. From there I could make the four feet to the drainpipe.

These were doubts running through my head as I shuffled into the yard: 1. Could I do it? 2. Would the pipe hold my weight? 3. Would the guttering hold? This was a Victorian guttering structure. Would it be able to hold me? It was 150 years' old and crumbling. Oh well, no time to ponder ifs and buts now, be positive. Get it done, my son. Where's your British bulldog spirit? He who dares and all that bollocks. Just do it.

A guard was stood very close to the toilet, too close for comfort. He would definitely be able to grab my swinging legs, drag me down and hold me until the others arrived to kick the shit out of me. The very thought of it bought me out in a cold sweat. Fuck it, I'll hit him first. I rushed at him and BANG! Over he went and up went the whistles. Alarm bells immediately went off, there were shouts – 'Oh no, the roof!' – and all hell broke loose. I dived onto the window bar then over to the pipe. I had made it, but now I had the long climb up the pipe. Now I know how Incy Wincy the fucking spider felt!

Towards the top I could see through the top window, looking into Ward Three. I clocked some guards. It was an office window. But I wasn't safe yet, the worst had to be conquered. The guttering structure, when I finally reached it, looked even more fragile than I had imagined. And it was fucking crumbling. Fuck me, this really could be Block 8, 'cos if it comes away it's taking me with it. What if it falls on top of me? Tons of Victorian brick coming down on my crust. I grabbed it and up I went. I heard a creak. Fuck me, it's coming away from the structure. It was like something out of a cartoon, except I wasn't fucking laughing and I didn't have as many lives! Block 8, here I come.

How I made it up to the top is still a miracle to this day. I looked up at the sky and laughed. I could see down below they were running around like lunatics. Little ant-like figures in chaos. 'Oi cunts, who's the daddy now?' I shouted out. Yeeeehoooooow. Yippppeeeee! I was dancing and shouting. I was elated. I had only gone and done it again. Once you can put down to luck, twice is the work of a mastermind. Unique. 'Anyone for tennis?' From my viewpoint I could see people coming in through the gates. It was about 1pm and visits were due to start soon. I actually clocked Ron Kray's mum Violet and brother Charlie. Violet Kray was a lovely lady. Her and Charlie always used to leave me a box full of goodies, cakes, pies, etc. after their visits. I shouted over to them and they waved. Violet shouted 'You be careful up there.' (What a typical thing for a mum to say, eh?)

A guard appeared at the top window and shouted at me 'What's the protest? What are your demands?' I laid it in the level with him. 'Right. You have my word, no destruction. Let the visits take place, 'cos Ron's Mum and brother are over there. If you stop the visits I will smash this roof AND the Norfolk roof off now. Your shout… now fuck off. Oh, and get me some food and drink.'

I wasn't expecting anything but I actually got a plastic bag passed out to me, containing lots of goodies. The visits went ahead while I caught up on some well-deserved sunbathing and ate and drank the supplies they'd given me, lapping it up like Lord of the Manor. At 4pm the visitors all filed out and as they left, Violet and Charlie shouted up to me and waved. At precisely 4.05pm I started my demolition act. Almost two and a half years of pure hatred poured out of me that day. THIS roof protest would be one that these bastards would never forget. It was meant to be. I was now going to make my mark in Broadmoor's history, and become a part of it. It felt magnificent, special and so wonderful. Every flying slate was a victory punch in the asylum's head to me. Every Broadmite in the last 150 years would shake my hand and salute this act of madness. The guards were by now shouting up from the windows, telling me what they intended to do when I came down. 'We're gonna break your fucking legs', 'I'll break your neck Peterson'… and threatening to torture me. Nasty fuckers. They should go on an anger-management course.

The Broadmites in Essex Block were getting fed up too. The loons in Essex were institutionalised, very settled and content with their lot. Most were very old and close to the end of life's struggle. So my protest was very disruptive to their routine and their lives. Imagine a young prick like me up on the roof, upsetting their routines, routines they relied on for any semblance of sanity. Sure they loved me, and they would have loved to have done what I was doing thirty years earlier, but they had only dreamed of it. They feared the consequences, so had never attempted something so dangerous. But truly they should have done it because they were all still here and fuck-all had changed for any of them. The only change was their hair was whiter. They were still Broadmites, the same as me. My brothers.

Guess what I could see up on the Norfolk Block roof? Come on, have a guess. I bet you can't. I could see York House and into the cell windows. It was the pussycat dolls. They were all at their windows, waving and cheering! 'Come on, show us your arse! Show us your willy!' I stripped off and shouted 'Yarhoooo, clock this!' Everyone was laughing and happy. It was a fucking brilliant moment. Roll on tonight when it's dark, I thought. I'd be able to see them better. But for now it was a while off and I had work to get done. Business before pleasure, girls. Yarhooooo. Yippppeeeee!

I aimed the slates at the guards, anything that moved – whizz – I skimmed a slate at it. Every one was a hundred and eighty and I had some beautiful hits. Windows, a van, a food trolley. On the end of Norfolk I could reach my old dormitory windows. I got plenty of a hundred and eighties with that lot. It felt so fucking good. The entire system was on its knees, again. The damage alone was astronomical. Big bucks. That's how to hurt a ruthless, evil system – in the pocket. Hit 'em hard. No amount of damage would make up for the decades of misery they had poured on sick people like myself. The torture they had used, and continued to use under people like Dr Loucas. The legalised murder of people who had no families, no relatives. The Kent House Broadmites were cheering, as were the Dorset loons. Every chicken in the cuckoo house was clucking!

Eventually Norfolk and Essex Houses were evacuated. I started throwing slates when the loons had moved. I had to – they were my brothers in arms. We were a family, a big family. Broadmoor is a brotherhood, believe me. And on that day I felt like… how shall I say it? The Daddy. The Governor. Daddy Broadmite. I don't want you to think I'm blowing my own trumpet. (Best you ask them who I am, let the loons decide!) But I saw myself as something of a union rep, their mouthpiece. It was time to let our grievances be known and if no one else was brave enough to stand up and do it, it was down to me. 'And you cunts are going to listen,' I thought.

I wanted to be a small part of making a change in Broadmoor. The mental and physical abuse had to be exposed in order for it to stop. The drug control needs to be looked into. And we demand more apple pies… and chocolate truffles. And at Christmas it's only fair we be allowed a bottle of brandy. And how about some sex?! If not with our sister Broadmites then why not allow us a prostitute once a month? Why not? What harm could it do? Listen, gays have sex in every institution around the world, a blow job here, a wank there, a quickie over there. This is actually discrimination against heterosexuals, is it not? Gays are very lucky in prison; they must be like a kid in a sweetshop. Well, it's not any fun for us straight chaps, you know. We get frustrated. We long for a bit of pussy. So how about it. (Could this actually be a human rights issue?)

I admit, at this time I was still not able to shoot my coco, it just wasn't happening. On a scale of one to ten my sex drive was zero. Yeah, that bad. And when I did manage to get a hard-on, I'd be pulling it so long I'd get bored. I really had dried up. My nuts weren't producing any juice and it really was starting to worry me. Well, this night was going to be memorable for more than just ripping off the roof.

At around 9pm, dusk was settling over the asylum and as the lights dimmed, I could see all the female Broadmites in their cells, all of them. Some were dangling their legs through the bars, making rude comments; others were flashing their tits at me. I saw one bend over (fuck me, she was using a vibrator!). I could barely believe my eyes. It was like my own private sex show. Insanity at its very best, but it really did stir my loins. I had the biggest hard-on since my wedding night. Come on, you know what's coming? (Excuse the pun)! I just had to… and did. Who cares who sees me, I'm going for it. No joke, I shot enough spunk to fill a yoghurt pot. It almost blew my balls off. I had never had a ham shank like that. I saw that moment as a turning point in my journey. Hey, I had three more wanks that night and I slept like a baby. It truly felt wonderful. This was heaven, it don't get no better than this, wanking on the asylum roof. Living the dream. They do say keep your dreams close or they will slip away. I'm so blessed, I really am. Fuck Block 8, I'm not ready to die, not yet. Tomorrow's a new day, a wrecking day. I've a job to finish off.

The wanking stops here, gotta get serious now. No time for weakness. Men who wank go blind, and who needs that? Pass the apple pies. It's a woman I need. I'll go to Block 8 willingly if you let me have a woman to love. Deal? No deal. Right, your roof's going. You'll pay for my loveless existence, you cruel fuckers. Night-night, I'll be back. I cuddled up with a ghost on the maddest roof in the world, and it's insanity.

CHAPTER 8

UP ON THE ROOF: PART II, DAY 2

(20 JUNE 1983)

'Never kiss a crocodile on the nose.
It will snap your head off, make no mistake about it!'

od, I feel good. Surprisingly I feel no dampness or aches or pains, I feel strong and ready for another day of destruction. A nice early start, like a farmer, (they work so hard them farmers). Well, so do us roofers! Crash! Bang! Wallop!

Then the bacon and onion fry-ups started. How predictable. Crafty fuckers. If that's not torture, what is? I'm bloody starving too. I always am. I wonder what's going on in the governor's office, with the officials all having their emergency meeting. 'What do we do now boys? What do we do with this lunatic? We can't have any more of this madness. He's making us look like a bunch of idiots. I'll tell you what we do with him. Block 8.'

I bet they were planning their retribution the second I came back down to terra firma. 'Let's drug him up so bad he won't know his arse from his elbow. Crack him like a walnut, make him crawl for

BROADMOOR HOSPITAL

SERIAL A: № 42

INCIDENT / CASUALTY REPORT

Date of Incident / ~~Casualty~~ JUNE 19th 1983

Time of Incident / ~~Casualty~~ APPROX. 2·30AM.

Location NORFOLK HOUSE AIRING COURT.

Name(s) of Patient(s)	Hosp. No.	House	Ward	RMO
PETERSON. M	M347	NORFOLK	III	DR LUCAS

Description of Events leading to Incident/~~Casualty~~

PATIENT RAN TOWARDS FOOTBALL WHILST ON AIRING COURT.

Description of Incident/~~Casualty~~ and extent of any Restraint used

PATIENT ON REACHING FOOTBALL JUMPED OVER IT & CONTINUED RUNNING to THE BACK OF THE TOILET, CLIMBED THE WINDOW OF THE N'O's OFFICE, ON TO THE TOILET ROOF, UP THE DRAIN FILTER PIPE AND ON TO THE ROOF, ADMIN INFORMED IMMEDIATELY, REST OF PATIENTS RETURNED TO WARD.

PATIENT STATED TO S/No BROOKS, S/No NORTH, N/o NORGATE, N/o BARON, & MYSELF THAT IF HE WAS GIVEN FOOD + WATER IT WOULD BE A PEACABLE PROTEST, IF NOT HE WOULD TAKE THE ROOF O' ESSEX + NORFOLK, FOOD + SQUASH PASSED TO PATIENT WHO SETTLED DOWN.

Witnesses to Incident	Discipline	INDIVIDUAL REPORT ATTACHED YES/NO	Signatures of Witnesses
PATIENT SETTLED	DOWN	AT TIME OF	REPORT.
S/N PETHICK.	S/N	No	A. Pethick
N/A SCOTT.	N/A		
ST/N IBBOTSON	ST/N		
SEN MEPHAM	SEN		

Injuries sustained by Staff: NONE
Patients:

Damage caused to Property: SEVERAL ROOF TILES TAKEN UP.

How was Incident Resolved: VISITED BY A/M/D. DR LE COUTER.

Signature : MO Attending _____ RMO _____

Senior Staff on Duty : _____

Discipline : S/N.

M.81

Incident Report Form about the second roof protest.

forgiveness. My beautiful roof, what a travesty! A fucking lunatic bringing all this misery and destruction.' Even Hitler's bombs didn't do the damage I had caused. Over a hundred years of peace in their institution and I turn it to jelly in two days. I wonder if they were considering using the ECT treatment on me by this stage, without the muscle relaxants or anaesthetic. What about a straight frontal lobe lobotomy? (Do you know, I think they would have, had I not had a strong family unit and close friends… and known contacts in the underworld). I knew they were fuming. 'He has us in a catch-22 situation, over a barrel. What if he makes it up there a third time? Impossible. We cannot allow that to happen. Move him? But where to? Nobody in their right mind would accept a problem like him. The prison system's washed its hands of him.'

Now it was time for them to have a huge fucking psychological problem, instead of dishing it out to the sick and vulnerable Broadmites like me. I once said, and I quote, 'A man's never lived until he's been in a straitjacket.' And I'd been in several, many times. I knew how they viewed me, and what they thought of me: 'He seems to enjoy the bad times more than the good.'

My journey was one of mass destruction. I was in and out of padded cells, strong boxes, cages, strip cells and body belts. I'd had forcible injections, three times the medication I should have been given – what else could they do to me that they hadn't already done? I think sometimes they hoped I'd top myself, take my own life like some of the other loons. Let me tell you this much, if ever I was found hanging, or mysteriously dead with a suicide note next to me, then some fucker's finished me off. The investigation would be so big they would be put under a microscope, and that was the last thing they wanted. 'No, he's not the sort of loon to take his own life, his family know that and so does everyone else.'

It was going to be back to seclusion for me, for a very, very long time. I had now become a serious problem to the institution and was coming close to exposing their practices and procedures. What the fuck do I care? Loneliness is only in one's mind; the shadow of friendship will never leave you. I sat it out another day, feeling the fresh air blow across my face, watching night time fall and listening to the sounds of nature, feeling as free as a bird.

CHAPTER 9

UP ON THE ROOF: PART II, DAYS 3 AND 4

(21–22 JUNE 1983)

'Never turn your back on a lunatic – unless you want
to be wearing him on your back!'

By Day 3, I was running out of gas. I was feeling tired and worn out. They had called my family again. Dad arrived on his own this time (I think Mark was on HMS *Illustrious* at this time) and John was abroad. The old fella looked a bit fed up.

'Come on son, you've done it this time. You've gotta come down sooner or later, you can't stay up there forever.'

'I can!' I bellowed down to him. I could see he was worried. 'Don't be silly son, come down.' I tried to explain to him, even though I was mentally and physically shattered. 'What for, dad? I'm tired of it. Tired of their shit. They're a bunch of cunts dad. Evil. They treat us like shit. It's all illegal, what they're doing here. They torture people, defenceless people. Look dad, I'm not being nasty but go home. This is my war, you don't understand.' He started to back off. 'I'll be back son', and with that he left. I watched my lovely dad walk away, through the gate lodge and into the car park. I shouted out, 'I love you dad.' And with that, he drove off. I cried my heart out. I don't mind admitting it. I did. That was a horrible, wicked thing to do to a wonderful dad. He did not deserve that. I cried so much I had nothing left inside but hate. I was a nasty, vicious fucker and Block 8 was the best thing for a nasty little cunt like me.

Right, let's go to work. There's lots more slates to smash. And beams. And pipes. And electrical wiring. Fuck the asbestos, I hope it kills me. Yaarhooooo! I was burning in the midday sun. What a tan I was getting. True to his word, dad returned the next day. I should tell you all now, when he comes it is because Broadmoor have called him, and they paid all his expenses and hotel bills. So in a way, it's like a mini hospital for the old rascal. 'I'm back son,' he said, giving me a reassuring smile. 'I knew you would be, you old git!' I said. He asked me again if I was coming down. I decided I had had my lot. 'Yeah, I've had my fill of it, dad. I'll come down. But I want half an hour with you, and some fish and chips and a jug of sweet tea. OH! And tell those cunts to stay well clear of me.'

The governor took care of my requests and said I could also phone my mum when I came down. Phone calls in those days were so rare they were virtually unheard of, so it was a nice squeeze for me. This time I climbed down through the attic on a ladder they put up. You should have seen their faces. If looks could kill I was a dead man walking. I was led into an office where Dad was standing with a few officials. They passed me the phone. It was Mum on the end of the line. It felt lovely to hear her warm voice too. 'Alright mum? Don't worry, it's all cool. Dad's here. He's promised me no more trouble! Ha ha. We're just gonna have a visit then I'll send him home. Love ya mum.' Click. The Duchess was okay.

But then dad told me the bad news. All the local and national media had covered my roof antics and were calling me the 'mad killer on the roof'. It had really hurt Mum because people were stopping her in the street and asking 'Eira, who did your boy kill?' Not a nice thing for any mum to have to put up with. Obviously it's libellous and a serious defamation of character, but you can't get legal aid to fight libel. Plus, who really cares in the general reading public; it didn't matter if I was a mass killer or a terrorist. I was a Broadmite, a madman, so no one gave a fuck. That was enough for them, and the media. It's catch-22 and you're fucked. Shortly after dad left the shit started again.

I got my fish and chips. They were all over the cell floor, and I quickly followed it – being slung in and threatened. It was to be expected. I had obviously upset their little apple cart. The consequences of my actions were only ever going to be negative. Mind you, I still ate the fish and chips. I then sat and waited for that slag Loucas to stick his head in my cell, to hear what immortal words of wisdom he would have for me. 'You'll never do that again. Not a third time.' Bang! My door slammed shut. 'FUCK OFF!' I shouted. 'Go on, fuck off. Go play with your pills.' There was no love lost between us. Hatred is a passion and it can burn in your heart. It's fuel to keep a man going in times of great stress and tribulation. I covered myself up in my blanket and fell into a deep sleep. My last thought as I drifted off was 'What next?' What the fuck comes after the storm? I slept like a baby.

In the morning my door flew open and they rushed in and injected me. I don't know why, I only knew it wasn't a good time. And believe me, no matter how tough you may think you are, toughness doesn't come into it when they rush you and stick a needle in your arse. These drugs could knock out a rhino. I just felt like 'Okay boys, do what you do best.' I drifted away into a crazy journey, a journey I had no say in. I had no control over anything. When I woke up (if I woke up), if they hadn't given me too much and caused an overdose as they'd done with others, I knew I would wake up in a pool of piss and sweat, and blood. You awake aching, drowsy, zombified with blurred vision and a dry mouth, a fucking total wreck.

It felt like I was going down a road in a car with no steering wheel, hoping I didn't crash. But you have to crash at some point, otherwise how do you stop? My whole life had become a danger zone, even from behind a locked door. Maybe I deserved it, and more, I don't know. But I just didn't care by now. It had gone too far for me. There was no way back. I was a lost man in the deepest, darkest hole in the entire penal system. I had buried myself, with a lot of help along the way from corrupt officials masquerading as professionals, doctors and medical experts. Could I ever fuck them up again? I doubted it. But that flicker of hatred hadn't been snuffed out. It still warmed my belly and my bowels and gave me that slither of fight I needed not to give up. If anyone could do it, it would be me. Don't back against me Broadmoor, because you will lose.

How I got through the next few months I cannot recall. It was just a drug-fuelled haze. I was out of it, mentally and physically. I used this time to reflect. I went within myself and searched for answers. I became a bit of a philosopher around this time of my life. A hermitised tortoise, the cell being my shell, my armour and my saviour. I no longer gave a fuck about what was happening outside of my space. What difference did it make to me? I never liked the godforsaken shit-hole or anything it stood for. My world was now this cell. I had my yoga, my workouts and my mind.

Books and magazines had now been passed as acceptable, so I got into some serious reading. I studied what I read and I began to follow politics. I found it interesting too. (Hey, do you know I have never voted? I am sixty-one years old now, and I have never voted. How many my age can say that?) I was enjoying my daily reads and my favourite paper was the *Express*. I liked their political pages, plus their sporting section wasn't too bad either (I'm a Spurs fan and I support my hometown club, Luton).

My days were flying by with little hassle as I was kept locked up and they left me alone. Don't get me wrong, this doesn't mean I was happy. But I was stress-free and I got my food, plenty of it. After several months of hostilities, the guards were being less militant with me; they just sort of dropped me out of it. I seldom saw the Broadmites. I did have the odd visit, but even they were getting few and far between. This was my choice; it's how I wanted it. I wanted to be alone, to have some peace. No stress, no worries.

Sadly, the bully boys still had to use bouts of brutality on some loons, and if it wasn't physical it was mental, threatening them if they didn't obey the rules. The threat of the unknown is worse than the actual act to some, and it places massive psychological stress on people. I heard shouts and screams, and could hear when they were dishing out a beating to some poor soul. I'd bang on my door or kick it repeatedly. 'Oi! You cunts kill him and you'll have ME in court telling everyone exactly what happened!' It always worked too. It was like a moment of realisation for them. Their bottle would go. They were the biggest fucking cowards on the planet, they stuck together like fucking bunches of grapes.

I managed to compile a second book of poetry, calling it *Solitary*. Guards Clive Mason and John Turner actually went out of their way to get it all typed up for me. (See, I told you there were some good eggs among the bunch. Some could be humane and respectful, and I never forget such things.) Thank you, guys. Mind you, they were still wankers at the end of the day to work in such a place, working among the shit, and allowing such brutality. Okay, so I know you're all dying to see another one of one of my poems. I shouldn't really; I should save them for a massive poetry collection. But what's one, eh? This one is called 'Padded Room'.

Padded Room

Fuck me, it's dark inside
My heart's gone to sleep
The walls have crushed my soul
A spider starts to creep

A cockroach on my face
slips inside my ear
it's gonna lay some eggs
My dreams turn to fear

What a fucked up life
Someone pass a blade
Cover me in roses
Smash me with a spade

Never touch my skin
Never kiss my lips
Never stroke my hair
Solitary always drips

Gone in a flash
Memories fade
Turn out the light
A crimson shade

Alone but happy
A world of make believe
Best say goodbye
It's not time to seed

You'd be amazed at how many of the loons suffer phobias. It's mental. Like the one who cannot walk on lines, any sort of lines (tiles, pavements, flooring). He thinks if he does he will die. Or the loon who eats peas and beans with a toothpick, one at a time. Or the one who can't wear any footwear at all in case he 'suffocates his feet'. He had only worn thick socks for twenty years, indoors and out. I told him, 'The socks are probably suffocating your feet more than shoes would.' Nope, he would have none of it, he'd made up his mind.

Others would sit in the day room counting the words that came up on the TV, furiously trying to add them up. If they didn't manage to add them up before the next advert they'd get agitated and annoyed with themselves. They'd sit there, furiously counting numbers on their fingers. Pure insanity! Some just can't relax or stop their minds racing; they are forever stressed out and strung out. One used to count the letters in pages of a book then recount it to make sure he had got it right. He'd do this with all books, all pages.

Some were cleanliness freaks, with undiagnosed OCD. We would call them the Germ Busters. You and I might wash our hands several times a day. A loon will scrub them in excess of one hundred times. I've seen them forever washing, scrubbing, brushing. One speck of dust and they would freak out to the point of a breakdown. It's crazy to see them panic so much over something so inconsequential. Then there were the mattress shaggers. Crazees who would bore a hole in their mattress, fill it with margarine and shag it. Over and over. Sickening and crazy but true, I assure you.

You cannot possibly relate to any of this because it's not something you have to witness, 'normal' people aren't thrust into this world and forced to watch this shit. Well, I was. I may have been violent but I was never mad, and if I had been I would have looked at all this madness around me and felt it was perfectly normal. Would you want an ex-Broadmite living next door to you? Well, would you? The stigma alone can spread fear. I personally believe that Broadmites are doomed to fail if they are ever released. (And no, I am *not* including myself in that. I am not a true Broadmite, in the real sense of the word.) Real Broadmites will have a relapse; they're bound to, because they're not normal people. How can they ever be? A breakdown for most people is a part of the process of life. In times of hardship or stress (losing a loved one or marriage breakdown), it happens for some. But if a psychopath or schizophrenic has a breakdown or neurosis, you had best not be near them, because they become lethal. You can't pacify a psycho, they're like a tornado – out of control.

It was around this time that I found a great comfort in nature. I studied spiders, ants, cockroaches – even the odd moth or ladybird. I had a pet spider and, as incredible as it sounds, I actually became close to it. When it ran off I really missed it. I used to watch it make a web up in the corner of the ceiling. Simple little things began to become gigantic to me in my insulated little world. I had what most free humans don't have, TIME, and I was in no rush.

Time to me was about making each day count, by turning a negative into a positive. Studying little critters became one way to focus and retain my sanity. Cockroaches click. It's their way of communicating. They amazed me, absolutely fascinated me. They ain't the nicest of creatures (okay, they're damned ugly). But ugly things are unique in their own way. Take the Elephant Man. Who don't love a freak? We all love a freak. That's one of the problems with society today. Political correctness gone mad. No more freak shows or dwarf-throwing events. The world's gone soft. 'You can't do this, you can't do that. That's bad for you, don't eat that, don't drink that.' I'll tell you what's bad for you. A cunt telling you what you can and can't do!

That next year seemed never-ending. I was glad to see 1984 roll in, but it was to prove no kinder than the previous year, although it started well when I got an encouraging independent psychology report from a consultant forensic psychiatrist at the Bethlem and Maudsley Hospital. Paul Bowden had done a full report on me and stated that my actions were a product of my environment and he felt that I had strong humanitarian grounds for early release from Broadmoor. Sadly, readers, Dr Loucas and his colleagues chose to ignore this report and buried it in my ever-growing file.

because the unit to which he would have to be transferred for a period before his discharge would not take him. An additional factor at this time was his longstanding complaint of ear symptoms which were not taken seriously and in the end were found to be due to a large abscess. And Mr. Peterson's notoriety continues to make him unacceptable to units at Broadmoor, other than where he is presently located on Norfolk House which provides only the most basic facilities and few, if any, priviledges. Other moves have been made to move Mr. Peterson from Broadmoor Hospital including attempts to have him charged with causing criminal damage in his last roof stripping escapade, or even resurrecting the assault charge which was adjourned sine die, so that he can serve a finite term of imprisonment.

As regards diagnosis, my view concurs with several of my colleagues that Mr. Peterson had a disorder of personality. For what it is worth I believe that it is the paranoid type with an excessive sensitivity to setbacks or what are taken to be humiliations or rebuffs. Experiences are interpreted with a hostile colouring and there is a combative and tenacious sense of personal rights. Mr. Peterson is excessively sensitive, aggressive and insistent. I do not subscribe to Mr. Peterson's view that his psychotic episodes were merely another example of his ability, to go to any lengths to achieve a change in his environment. Firstly the simulation of insanity is a most unlikely resort of someone steeped in criminal culture as is Mr. Peterson - it would be beneath him. Secondly, the symptoms which he says he fabricated bear no similarity to the ones he exhibited. I do think Mr. Peterson suffered a psychotic breakdown in the setting of a paranoid and aggressive personality disorder. I do not believe that he is schizophrenic and the liveliness, colour and flexibility of his personality are quite out of keeping with a schizophrenic process illness. In latter years Mr. Peterson has been the victim of other peoples' manipulations and he has in many senses become a hostage to his own notoriety.

Mr. Peterson's life is an almost daily struggle to exercise self control and with the exception of the episodes of criminal damange his behaviour latterly has been exemplary. It is he who has detached himself from the vicious circle of provocation and retribution but it seems that he is denied a more amenable and habilitative environment at Broadmoor, which his R.M.O. clearly considers he is suitable for, so he remains in an environment which provides only the most basic level of care. In fact Mr. Peterson has reached the stage where the staff's attitude to him is challenging and provocative and it is only with the greatest difficulty that he does not fulfil their prediction of further outrage.

My view is that Mr. Person's violence has been very much a product of the environment which is designed to contain him. There is no further evidence to suggest that its basis lies in an abnormality of brain functioning and other than to the extent that he is a run-of-the-mill criminal I would not expect his disorder of personality to present a risk to the community at large. Dr. Michael Craft from Garth Angharad Hospital saw Mr. Peterson at Broadmoor in December 1982 and it will be clear that he envisages Garth Angharad being a base for Mr. Peterson's continuing rehabilitation. I do not think that Broadmoor is or can provide a rehabilitative environment for Mr. Peterson and the time must have come for his discharge. I have some reservations about his suitability for a relatively small provincial 'semi' secure unit, which might offer particular temptations, and for his placement with his parents in the Aberyswyth Conservative Club but Mr. Peterson is confident that he would successfully reintegrate himself into society if allowed to follow this course.

Part of the independent psychiatric report on Charlie.

Re: Mickey PETERSON (cont'd)   - 4 -

Lastly, I believe that this is a most unusal case in that there are strong
humanitarian grounds for recommending Mr. Peterson's early release from
Broadmoor.

Paul Bowden
MPhil., MRCP., FRCPsych.
Consultant Forensic Psychiatrist

Bethlem Royal and the Maudsley Hospital
and to the Home Office

It had also been a cold Christmas and there was no heating in Norfolk
Block. I wrote and complained repeatedly about the lack of heating.
It was so bad I even wrote to my local MP.

Some of the poor old boys on the ward nearly fucking died it was
so cold. It was totally inhumane. Mad or not, everyone is entitled
to basic food and warmth. Even prisoners got better treatment than
us. Do you know what their answer was? To give us an extra blanket
each. What a total piss-take.

NoTe.
You will TAKe -
- YouR MeDicATioN

Mr M Peterson
73478
NORFOLK WARD 2

15.12.1983

Dear Mr Peterson

As Secretary to the Hospital Management Team, I am
writing to advise you that the Team have considered
your letter of 3 December 1983, regarding the lack
of heating in the rooms in Norfolk House, at night.

I am advised that patients have been provided with
new wool blankets, to help with this problem — more
cannot be done because of the age of the present
central heating system and the hospital's Redevelopment programme, I regret.

Yours sincerely

Mary Lane (Mrs.)
Secretary
Hospital Management Team

Broadmoor's response to the heating complaint.

When January arrived I actually thought, 'Let's just have a happy year.' So I plodded on regardless. Do you know, it took the authorities almost a year to repair the damage I'd done? All the fixing and banging was driving us all mad. The hospital had by now appointed a new superintendent, a Dr Hamilton. He had been my old quack when I was on Kent Block. I didn't hate him, but I couldn't respect the man. For me, a proper man has to be a leader of men. A man who would lead his men into war. I saw Hamilton as a regimented disciplinarian – a wimpish prat. I couldn't abide him.

I'd even met prison governors who I hated but ultimately respected. I'd attacked a lot of governors throughout my mad journey, and I'd been kicked up and down dungeons for all of my adult life, in some of the toughest jails in England, but I believe each jail has to have its leader, a fair man. A man of credibility. And men like Hamilton couldn't run a piss-up in a brewery. He would make a decision and then change it a few days later. He would say something and then go against it at the drop of a hat. I couldn't respect that, and because of it, I didn't like him. It was nothing personal… yet. But it would come, no doubt.

As April rolled on, my family were becoming increasingly concerned for me. My visits had been stopped, for no reason other than vindictiveness. I then had a tribunal that turned out to be a complete fucking farce. Not one of the thirteen family members who turned up was allowed inside, and Dr Loucas had an open forum to talk about me. According to my mother, he seemed to suggest that my parents were terrified at the thought of me returning home. What a load of all bollocks. My dear old dad wrote an impassioned letter to Hamilton, and told him who he thought was to blame for my poor state of mine: that evil swine Loucas.

19th April 84

Conservative Club.
Eastgate St.
Aberystwyth.
Dyfed.

BROADMOOR HOSPITAL
GENERAL
19 APR 1984
OFFICE
RECEIVED
7347

Dear Sir,
I am the Father of M. G. Peterson who at this moment is in Norfolk I. His Mother and I are very upset to think that his relatives have been stopped from visiting him. This to me is ridiculous, to punish them for something they no nothing about is beyond reason. It's not all Michaels fault that he is in the position that he is in to-day. I blame Dr. Loucas. and so long as my Son is under him he will get nowhere. If he had a

Charlie's dad's letter to the hospital.

little compassion and treat him like a human being instead of an animal then I'm sure, things would be a lot different. I'm not asking you I am pleading with you to do your best to get Michael transferred to another unit for his sake as well as ours, as I know that he will not accept the conditions he is existing under at the present time. Please do your best.

Thank you.

Yours Sincerely.

Mr. J. Peterson.

I also wrote a full statement, exposing their lies and bollocks.

However, April showers always bring a rainbow. Please let it shine on me. All that wonderful colour. Let me have some! It was just a lucky day, too lucky to be true. There was no way I could have planned this spectacular event. Some things just occur out of the blue. Like a spontaneous beautiful act, like an orgasm, a rush of adrenalin –and suddenly, there's fucking magic!

CHAPTER 10

ROOF III: MY HAT-TRICK (GIVE ME THE FUCKING BALL!)

(14 MARCH 1984)

'Who teaches birds to build a nest?
What came first, the bird or the egg?
I wish I knew!'

I am heading out to the little yard but the lock on the door is busted. Fucked. The guard said to the other one holding me, 'Stick him out on the big yard.' The guard looked at me and then his colleague. 'But the scaffolding is still up.' Another guard said, 'So what? It's got twenty-foot tin sheets up it. A monkey couldn't get up there.' 'Fucking hell' I thought, 'I am here you know, talking about me as though I was the cat's mother'.

They dithered over whether it was safe to let me out on the big yard, talking among themselves as though I was the Invisible Man. 'Fuck it, make your minds up,' I thought to myself. They stuck me out on the big yard, the same yard I had bolted from before. Surely I couldn't do it again. Could I? I clocked the tin sheets all around the block, protecting the scaffolding. Impossible. No way. Six guards came out and stood in their respective places, strategically placed as ever. I shuffled around trying not to look excited. My mind is racing. Could I? Should I? SHALL I? Fuck it, the temptation was too much. If I didn't go for it I knew I would regret it for the rest of my life. Then again, if I fail I'm fucked big time, more years of emptiness. What could I do? What should I do? FUCK IT!

I sprinted. I went for it, shit or bust. My right foot hit the tin sheet, which stretched six feet up. I somehow bent it enough to get my fingers to the edge at the top, and climb up a few feet. The guards were jumping, trying to grab my feet. I went up a few more feet and the guards started shouting out to the roofers above me. 'RUN! QUICK! GET DOWN, HE'S COMING UP!' Ha ha. Abandon ship!

They scattered down a ladder leading back inside to the ward. Suddenly my fingers got trapped. I couldn't hold on. I was sure it was over for me. (Fuck me, thwarted before I'd even got halfway.) This was surely a bridge too far. But then my weight started to bend the tin inwards and I could see the boards and scaffold poles behind it. My fingers were pouring blood but they were freed and I scrambled on to the platform. I had made it. I screamed out, 'Yeah, you leg it cunts 'cos I'm back.'

My hat-trick. My Geoff Hurst. My World Cup. Charlie fucking Bronson does it for England and Loons United. You couldn't make this shit up. 'Look at me Ma, top of the world!' And I've now got planks, scaffold bars, even ladders to play with. What a complete security fuck-up. The workmen were just days away from dismantling and removing the scaffolding and metal sheeting when I struck. The phones would by now be on fire. 'He's back up in the roof! Evacuate the building, call the police, call the fire brigade, we have an emergency!' I bet headquarters were shaking their heads. 'How the fuck have they allowed this to happen, AGAIN? Get that prick Hamilton on the phone now.' I bet Dr McGrath was fucking glad he retired when he did now!

Incident Report Form about the third roof protest.

Of course, the media loved it. Bit of drama, bit of danger, lots of sensationalism for them to report, with the fictitious 'spokesman' to give them a quote. Me, a loon, had got the authorities by the balls... again. Even I'd thought it would be impossible, and yet here I was.

And like an old friend, the rainbow came back to smile on me. I couldn't believe it, it was déjà vu, a miracle. This rainbow must love me. Shine on, you beauty. In fact, come on, open up and piss all over me. Come on, I can't be beaten. Ronnie Kray once called me 'The Uncrowned Champ'. Well, crown me. I AM the King of the Asylum. Unbeatable. Five years of shit and I am still here and I am still kicking. Five years of my life squeezed dry in this hellhole. Well, now I am the No. 1 Broadmite of all time. Nobody could beat my record. It's in the history books, boys, read it. Study it. I made criminal history. I was the top nut. You fuckers created what you see before you, and now you don't know how to handle me. Ha ha ha ha ha ha ha. It's 1984 and it's mine! Who cares any more? I don't.

I had a surge of adrenalin that made my heart feel tight. 'Fuck me,' I thought. 'Not a stroke, surely not.' I had to sit down and take a deep breath in. It was all too much for me. The excitement, the achievement, the insanity of it had caught up with me. This was a dream come true, like winning ten million on the lottery. I fell in love with the whole madness of life. I actually felt so overwhelmed I was in a state of shock. The only way I can describe my feelings is to say that it felt like I'd been plucked off the ground by some spaceship, taken out of the hellhole I was living in, and transported to the roof for some serious entertainment.

Suddenly I was feeling peckish. I shouted down, 'Get Hamilton over here, lively. I want to see the superintendent right now. You've got twenty minutes or the roof comes off.' It took him ten. Pronto he appeared at the top window as I sat on the scaffolding, a big smile on my face.

'Pen and paper,' I said. 'What?' he asked. 'I said get a fucking pen and paper now, you cunt!' A guard passed him both. 'Okay Doc,' I instructed, 'write this down.' I then reeled off my list. 'Bag of chips, a pizza, a bottle of Coke, a cake, some fruit, a bag of nuts, some crisps. Get it?' He looked concerned: 'Are you going to take the roof off?' I wasn't in the mood for questions and as far as I was concerned, he wasn't in the position to be asking them. 'No, I've got a lighter. I'm gonna burn it down if I don't get that order. Now fuck off and don't come back without my grub.' I never had a lighter but what's a little fib between friends? I'm sure God will forgive me.

So there I am, and there I sat, waiting. The Broadmoor officials are praying for a peaceful end, one that ends with their roof in one piece. Fuck me, I'm in a nice position here. Shall I strong it and demand a blow job off Mary Whitehouse?!

Half an hour later, maybe forty-five minutes, and Dr Hamilton returns with my goodies and they are passed up to me. 'Right, this is how it works,' I advise them. 'I'm off for a picnic. They'll be no damage or flames. I will be back later.' He asked me when. 'When I'm ready! Don't get lemon with me; I'm the daddy, not you. You do as you're told. Best you don't upset me. I'll be back when I'm ready. Meantime, fuck off and start praying. Oh, and don't forget to bring the pen and paper for my next order when you come back. Adios amigo!'

I sat against the scaffolding and enjoyed my little picnic, enjoying this amazing moment. It takes a while for it to sink in when you realise you have the power, that you are suddenly the one holding the aces. For once I actually had this bunch of shit where I wanted them, right by the short and curlies. To say there'd been a shift in power is an understatement. I had them in the palm of my hand. I could see just outside the wall that the press and TV people had started congregating; they were waiting patiently behind the barriers the police had erected, trying to find out the latest. I decided to give them a bit of verbal. Well, it was all they expected of a madman like me. The scum had called me a 'murderer' in previous media coverage, a 'killer'. What about the upset it had caused my family, my mother? That's libel.

Anyway, who am I to deny our great British public a story? It was my duty to get it out there to people, let it be known exactly what Broadmoor stood for, what went on behind closed doors. This was my platform to the world. After all, I am the Broadmite spokesman (self-appointed, I admit). And I wasn't a bad one, if I say so myself. Come on, who would you prefer – me or Arthur Scargill? Me, every time. So I gave it my best shot.

'Oi, yes it's me, your friendly loon. King of Broadmoor. Please don't call me a killer this time. Sure I've come close once or twice but so did my granny with the pools. Nearly is not good enough. Now I've cleared that up, let's get on with it. I'm up here protesting about the guards' brutality against us defenceless loons. It's barbaric. And the porridge is cold and lumpy. Our mattresses are damp. There's no heating in our cells and the showers are cold. We demand a public enquiry. We demand some human rights. We want some pussy time. And I want a TV in my cell and a coffee percolator. Why can't we have a coach trip to Blackpool or a day out at Ascot Races? We demand some humanity.'

Fuck it, they're not even listening to me. I even heard one shout out, 'Who do you think you are, you nutter?' Nice. Is that any way to speak to a Broadmite legend? If that's all the thanks I was going to get then they could all fuck off! Would they have treated Scargill like that? Gutless, spineless cunts. All they wanted was sensationalism and lies. 'Don't call me a killer again or I'll do the lot of you. Go on, fuck off. Us loons don't need you fucking hypocrites.'

I then mooned them for good measure. 'FUCK OFF!' I was bored now and in need of some serious action. Broadmoor's appointed head prat appeared back at the window with his pen and paper ready. 'I never called you, Hamilton.' He was trying to appease me. 'I thought you might like to talk.' This only angered me. 'You've had five fucking years to talk to me.' He persisted. 'Look I may have a deal for you. Up to now you've done no damage. You've been true to your word. So let's talk. What is it you want?' He's asking me what I want! Lovely words, I like it. I had a think about it for a few seconds.

'Er... what have you to offer? Go on, make me an offer I can't refuse.' He shouted up without hesitation: 'Well, what about a transfer?' I have to admit, it got my attention. 'I'm listening,' I said, 'go on.' He asked me what I would think to a move to Ashworth Hospital, in Liverpool. 'Look Hamilton, cut the shit. It's Ashworth ASYLUM, not Hospital. Next you'll be telling me the guards are nurses. And I'm a pumpkin.'

He went on to tell me that Ashworth is very modern, a new place with a new design. 'Like what?' I asked. He then gives me the brochure spiel on the place. 'It has an indoor swimming pool, a gym and the rooms are comfortable.' I was going nowhere, so I let him continue. 'You'll have a lot more freedom too.' I asked when I could go. 'Within a week or two,' he assured me. I wanted out NOW. 'What about now, TODAY?' I asked. He said it was impossible and the soonest he could expedite the move would be a week. 'Seven days?' I asked. 'Yes, seven days and you'll be swimming. A nice comfortable room, a gym, and lots of good food.' This would need some serious consideration. 'Go get me a mug of tea with two sugars. I need to think about this. Oh, and some custard creams.' Hamilton sent a guard off to sort it. ('There were no custard creams, would chocolate bourbons do?')

So there I am, sat atop Broadmoor's roof, dunking my bourbons into a mug of tea and dwelling over what seems like a very tempting deal. Too tempting to resist. It was a deal I would have been crazy to refuse. I was a loon, not crazy! If I refused and ripped the roof off I faced more years of shit. What should I do? What would any sane person do? 'IT'S A BLOODY DEAL HAMILTON.' I clambered down to the window, reached out and looked him in the eye and we shook on it.

'Just one thing before I come in,' I said. 'Write down all our grievances, so all this shit in Norfolk Ward stops.' He nodded his head. 'Okay, we can do that.' I asked him if he'd phoned my dad and he assured me he hadn't. He asked me to wait until he'd got his staff in position to meet me at the bottom of the scaffolding before I climbed in. Getting his bully boys in position, no doubt. He promised me there would be no funny business. All would be cool and done properly. He told me I would be led back to my cell and locked up, and he would then start the paperwork for my move. It all sounded good to me... too good maybe.

'Okay, when you're ready, make your way down,' he said. I have to say, it was an easier climb down than it had been going up. Well, as soon as my feet hit the ground I was grabbed by too many hands to distinguish how many guards it was. I was punched, kicked AND strangled. Yes, strangled. Someone had me in a stronghold round my neck. They dragged me off to my cell and I was slung in like a rag doll. I could taste that familiar iron taste of blood in my mouth, trickling down my throat.

I was fuming. So much for trusting a man, for taking his word and his handshake as gospel. He had fucked me big time. The lying, spineless cunt had pulled one over on me. I could not fucking believe it. I should have known not to trust the sewer rat. I went against my OWN golden rule for survival, never to believe a word these people say, or to trust it. What a bloody mug I had been. Now what? Yeah, like I didn't fucking know already.

CHAPTER 11

SECLUSION

'It's all mind over matter. I don't mind
and fuck-all ever matters!'

In his book, *Inside Ashworth*, editor and professor of mental health policy, David Pilgrim, states: 'In hospitals rather than prisons there is a particular duty of care to ameliorate mental distress. Health care should not aggravate distress by denying the patient access to ordinary human contact. Solitary confinement inflicts this distress. Using the euphemism of "seclusion" does not alter this fact.'

Further, he says, 'locking them up indefinitely in an institution, which largely functions as a prison but is called a "hospital", is one-dimensional and unimaginative. It is costly in time and money, and constricts the lives for all residents (and staff too, albeit to a lesser extent)'.

Home office *file*

BROADMOOR ~~HOSPITAL~~ *PRISON*
Crowthorne Berks RG11 7EG
Station: Crowthorne (Southern Region) *7347*
Telephone: Crowthorne (0344) 773111
OR GET IN TOUCH WITH THE P-O-A !!!

Peterson *73478*
Norfolk House *ISOLATION WING*
Ward 1 *CONTROL UNIT.*
CELL No 3.   Your reference *INMATE*
DOUBLE DOOR'S   Our reference *GOVENOR*

Date

6 April 1984

~~Dear Mr~~ Peterson

Thank you for your recent letters and I am sorry for
the delay in replying to you. I cannot accept the
charges you make at me and I hope you will realise
that as our contract was made under duress there may
have to be a delay in implementing it. I have not
ignored the comments and criticisms you made and we
are seeing what we can do about them. I personally
have not stopped any of your visits and you should
talk about them with Dr Loucas. I am discussing with
him the question of your possible transfer to Park Lane.

~~Yours sincerely~~

John R Hamilton

*You LIED me DOWN FROM THE ROOF !
You SHOOK ON A DEAL YOU HAD NO
INTENTIONS OF SEEING THROUGH !*

Hospital letter (and part of Charlie's reply) about the roof protest.

'I want to see Hamilton NOW! Now, you CUNTS! Get Hamilton here NOW!' He wouldn't come. What could he say? There was nothing more the heartless prick could say. He'd lied. Lied to save his roof and probably his job. Some might say he had no choice. I say a lie is a lie. And he fucking lied to me, the slag. Promising me a life of something better than this living hell, this 24-hour shit-hole. 'Right cunts, I am on hunger strike.' I'm not sure why I chose to starve myself. But I had said it and now I had to commit to it. A Broadmite's word is all he has and my word WAS my bond, unlike Hamilton, the slag.

I started my hunger strike and the way I felt, I was truly prepared to die. At least I'd be out of this living nightmare. Now this was one hell of a decision to make. Don't forget, this wasn't a prison. Unlike in prison, they could and DID force feed you. It is a mental institution and if they say you're not sane enough to think for yourself then they have the power to physically restrain you, ram a large plastic pipe down your throat and pour in liquids such as soup, Complan milks, etc. Cunts!

But they didn't come anywhere near me. I was waiting for it. Every day, every hour, every minute, I was on tenterhooks, on my toes, waiting for them to burst in. I was like a tiger, alert and ready for them to strike. But they never came, and neither did Hamilton. I drank water, but nothing else passed my lips. Let me tell you, a hunger strike is a torturous thing to inflict on yourself, especially for a man like me who loves his grub so much. It really is a last resort and I would NOT recommend it.

The guard John Turner came to my door most days. He was genuinely concerned for me. I think he was ordered to keep a check on me and report back to Hamilton... in case I died! I'm not silly – a fucking ant could work that out. But John was one of the very few decent guards, and he always made a bit of time for me. 'Look,' he advised, 'Hamilton won't see you while you make demands and threats. Come off the hunger strike and I'm sure we can sort this situation out.'

I was so angry and frustrated. 'Fuck off, you're only a message boy. Go and tell that cunt to get a body bag ready, 'cos I'm not coming out till I see that cunt! The little fat, lying prick. They're all the same them head shrinks. Well he's not playing games with my crust.'

I'm gonna tell you something now that you might find hard to believe. After the first three days of a hunger strike, it actually gets easier. Those first three days are murder. You're debating whether to eat your pillow. It turns into a giant marshmallow. Every single thought you have is about food, chewing a steak or peeling a juicy bit of fruit. It's horrible, sheer torture. After a week, you've cracked it really. Don't get me wrong, it's still not nice, but it is easier. Your stomach makes some very funny noises, I can tell you. Your arsehole dries up and your body feels really strange, like a shell. Your bones creak, your piss smells. Your eyes get blurry and tired for no reason. You are just not yourself, and you dream a lot. It's like being in a constant dream-like state. You sleep a lot, you forget things.

Suddenly the cell became very claustrophobic to me. I was restless, unsure. I remember forever having water passed through the hatch to me. Fuck me, I really was a candidate for Block 8 and my thoughts were getting stronger about seeing it through. I couldn't back down now. I used to go berserk (literally) when I smelled the grub being dished up for the other Broadmites. 'You're doing that on purpose. I hope you choke on it you fucking vermin!' Mr fucking Tortoise Man, me. My pride was going to be my downfall. I was killing myself. Trapped up in a shell with no escape.

Hey, speaking of which, did I tell you about the time I did try to escape? It was while I was on Norfolk Ward Three. I managed to get my hands on an angel wire, which is a kind of tungsten roller that cuts through metal. I also got hold of a car key, a screwdriver and some cash. Ask me no questions and I'll tell you no lies.

Now remember, at this time, when we went into our cells of a night we had to hand over all our clothing. We weren't allowed to take it in the cell with us. We'd undress and be handed our pyjamas. However, I'd also managed to procure a set of clothing and shoes. The first night, I worked the bars in half-hour shifts, jumping back into bed whenever the night watch passed to spy through the Judas Hole at me. I didn't have a watch at this time but I'd hear the chimes of the gate lodge clock, and whip sharpish back into bed. As I sawed away at the bar I held a blanket against it with my head, to muffle the noise. By 5am the bar was hanging by the smallest slither. I knew I could easily snap this with my hands so I left it. I decided I was going to feign sickness so I could stay in my room all day and reserve my strength for when the time came to make my getaway.

Well, what is it they say about the best-laid plans? The bastards weren't having any of it and insisted I get up and shower. While I was in the shower room they searched the cell and found my handiwork. Before I knew it they'd stopped all my visitors, with Loucas threatening to withhold all visits until I told him where I'd got the saw and other items. 'Go fuck yourself,' I told him, 'what are you going to do, stop me seeing anyone for thirty years. Fuck off you cunt!'

Anyway, we digress. I'm now near to death with my hunger strike and felt I didn't have long for this world. Suddenly he just appeared. Bang! Hamilton was at my hatch. It was day ten. By now I didn't care about his presence, he was just a blur to me. 'I've some good news for you. You'll be moving soon.'

I called him a liar. 'No, I'm not lying. You're being transferred to

Ashworth soon.' I'd heard his shit before. 'How do I know you're not lying again, just to get me to eat?' He passed me in an official letter from Ashworth stating that I'd be accepted. Fuck me, it was true. I was going. Ha ha ha. Hee hee hee.

'Pass me in some grub and fast!' Pies, bread, cakes, anything. I'd have eaten anything. I told them to get my chocolate bars and biscuits from my box, and sharpish.

Charlie's letter regarding his hunger strike.

I'm going to tell you something now about going on a hunger strike that will make your eyes water, as much as it did mine at the time. That first shit you have, after starving yourself, it's like giving birth to the biggest, hardest turd ever. Pain is not the word for it. It is agony, and a slow one at that. And it's even worse on a chamber pot! I don't mind admitting I screamed abuse as I passed that first turd. I think the entire Norfolk Block heard me as it squeezed out. Black Forest logs are not supposed to come out of there. Fuck me, I could have used this as a cosh against the guards! I even had to snap it off 'cos it was too long to fit in the pot. I'm sure it sounds funny now, but it was no joke, believe me.

Never again. Fuck them hunger strikes, they're for masochists. I'd prefer to be a sadistic bastard. I respect my body too much to kill myself off. It was now time to reflect and prepare for my transfer. I was going to a brand new asylum up north.

CHAPTER 12

REFLECTIONS OF MY MIND

'To be or not to be. Who gives a fuck? Pass the cheese rolls.'

My time at Broadmoor, as I was soon to discover, was now coming to an end. A Dr McCulloch came to see me from Ashworth. He was the superintendent there and I was told my doctor would be a Dr Hunter. McCulloch seemed sincere, even to a seasoned cynic like me. I gotta admit, it's gotta be said right now, I liked him. I could see he was a decent man, a good man. I told him about all of my struggles here, my personal hell, and he actually believed me. He knew, he really knew.

Broadmoor was and is just stuck in the nineteenth century. It hasn't moved or progressed at all. It's like a time warp, stuck in a Victorian era of ignorance, abuse and lack of understanding for mental health issues. Us Broadmites were just Victorian loonies, treated like imbeciles. It was the system that was insane, not us. We were just dragged into it – sucked in – and then we had the life sucked out of us. I know because I witnessed it for myself. I watched Michael Martin arrive a fit, young vibrant man, full of life and laughter, and they turned him into an overweight, lumbering, violent zombie. And then they choked him to death, MURDERED him because they couldn't cope with what they had created.

Well, this was now it for me, the end of the road. Had I won, or lost? Who could tell? I don't think it was about that for me; it was more a case of who was right and who was wrong. What could be learnt from it all? My next couple of weeks were ones full of reflection and deep thoughts. I had so much to think about. I felt like a little chick breaking free from the egg, a sense of victory within me. I don't want to get emotional about it but even now, all these years later, I feel those same feelings pull on my heart. I felt happy and it felt wonderful. I knew I was only going to another asylum but it still felt good. Little did I know that one day I would be famous for being the only loon to hit all three asylums' roofs (Rampton, Broadmoor AND Ashworth).

Rampton had been hell, Broadmoor was a world of insanity but I hoped Ashworth would be a five-star job. Sure I was saddened to be leaving my Broadmite brothers and sisters, but nothing lasts for ever, does it? Men have to march on and make new roads. Who wants to end up like a budgie in a cage, or a fish in a bowl, or a hamster on a wheel? Not me! Never. I'd done my bit for human rights and raised the profile of the loon, as well as the roof!

My old buddy Ronnie Kray plodded on there until he sadly died on 17 March 1995. A tragic end because he had deserved so much better. Reg Kray later wrote in his book *A Way of Life* that Ron had told him they had stopped his medication. For a schizophrenic, this must have been torture. Ron was also moved on to the dreaded Norfolk Ward. He deserved better than that. The only good thing I can say is that he escaped Block 8. He was loved and respected by his family and friends, so his body was released and he was given a proper East End funeral. A true Broadmite tribute; max respect to that.

So many more died, every one of them still in my heart. My memories flooded me with good thoughts. Like when Alan Reeve had it over the wall from Essex Block. Using a TV aerial, he managed to scale the wall, got clean away and totally disappeared. He jumped into a waiting car and had it sharpish to Dover. Sadly, he shot a copper dead in Holland and served fifteen years in a Dutch jail before being returned to the big house. Then there was Nobby Clarke. He garrotted a paedo in the showers with a banjo string. How we all cheered! I remembered child killer James Lang jumping over the wall and smashing his ankles back on 21 July 1981. 'Hooray!' We all cheered again. He was caught twenty hours later, thank fuck, nursing a broken ankle. Best thing for the nonce. He had killed a young teenage girl after raping her in the early 1970s. The beast.

I recalled Roy Shaw breaking a doctor's jaw, and Freddie Mills smashing his cell door clean off. Peter Cook put forty stitches in a guard's face. These were all the crazy, mad memories that made me smile. Fuck me, to think I've survived all that, not to mention my own madness. I loved them all. How could you not love such people, such survivors? Loons, doing things you cannot possibly comprehend. Your eyes don't believe it when they're actually seeing it. One loon coming out of the toilet, wrapped head to toe in bog paper like a mummy, jumping off tables in the dining room and smashing head first into things. Loons pulling their own teeth out, sewing their eyelids together, wanking away while they watched telly. The constant laughter, the tears, the sadness, the pain, the screams. It created a brotherhood, with companionship and closeness. The hugs of compassion and years of isolation.

Add it all up and it's a beautiful piece of humanity wrapped up in insanity. I loved it and I had been a part of it, and I am proud of it. It was my own sanctuary to my own sanity. I want to leave you, if I may, with a few of my favourite stories – my most memorable. If you don't read these and smile then you've no heart. Enjoy!

PART 2

OTHER MADNESS

CHAPTER 13

THE MANURE HEAP
AND OTHER MADNESS

'Madmen don't dream the dream. They live it!'

When I first landed in Broadmoor, on Somerset Block, we were allowed to exercise down on the field, and patients from all the other blocks would come out. There would be scores of us. On some weekends there would be a few hundred of us. All sorts of loonies. Fat ones, thin ones, black ones, ugly ones, a few hunchbacks, a couple of midgets even. A right assortment. The field was massive and there was a magnificent orchard too; it was beautiful. If the wall hadn't been surrounding us, it would have seemed like a beautiful park. Somerset had a football pitch, a cricket pitch, bowls, the lot.

Anyway, I'm walking around, taking it all in, and it felt great. I used to really enjoy that walk, the wind on my face, breathing in the clean air. But I was being stalked. Yeah, a fucking stalker. A little old loon with a tweed coat and a cap on. I walk, he walks. I stop, he stops. He's doing my fucking canister in. This went on for about twenty minutes, so eventually I marched up to him. 'What's your fucking game?! What are you following me for? Go on, fuck off!' If he was thirty years younger I'd have chinned the nutter. Off I walked. He followed me!

Now I'm getting mad. I shot round on him. 'LOOK! Fuck off before you end up in the hospital ward with a hole in your nut.' Then the insanity started. 'Will you take me with you?' he asked me. 'What? Take you where? What you on about?' I said. 'You're going to escape. I know you are. And I'm coming with you,' he bellowed. 'SHUT UP!' I hissed at him. 'What the fuck are you talking about? What you going on about?' I didn't have a clue what he was talking about. 'Who the fuck told you I'm gonna escape? Anyway, what's your game following me?'

He carried on. 'I just want to escape with you. Please don't leave me behind.' I asked him how long he'd been in Broadmoor. 'Thirty-five years,' he replied. 'Then why haven't you escaped yourself?' I asked. Do you know what he said? 'Because I've been waiting for you to take me.'

Fuck me, this was getting too much for me. I didn't need this bollocks. If the guards overheard this shit, the word 'escape', I'd be in for it. I'd be in isolation before my feet touched the fucking ground. He kept going on and on and on. 'Escape' this, 'escape' fucking that. I felt like strangling him. I finally had enough. 'Okay pop, look. I'll take you with me, okay? We are going over the wall together, tonight.'

He got as excited as a kid in a sweet shop. 'I KNEW IT. I KNEW IT.' I told him this was my plan. 'See that big pile of manure over there? Well, you go over there, dive in and cover yourself and just wait for me to come and get you. Got it? When the bell goes for us to go in, you stay covered and I'll come back with a ladder tonight. We'll be away.' He nodded excitedly. 'You won't forget me, will you?' he asked. 'Of course I won't,' I said. 'You're my right-hand man, you are!'

I never in a million years expected the old fart to actually do it. But he did. Off he rushed and buried himself in the fucking pile of manure. All I could see was his mad eyes staring out. As we were called in and I walked past the shit heap, I gave him the thumbs up and a wink. 'Stay there pop,' I hissed. 'I'll be about four hours.'

Obviously he was found eventually, after being discovered to be missing, and he immediately told the guards he was going over the wall with me. I got a serious pull on that. They quizzed me over a possible escape. I told them, 'Look, I've no plans to escape and if I DID have, do you really think I would take that old nutter with me?' They weren't happy with that answer. 'Well, did you tell him to hide?' I had nothing to hide myself. 'Yes, I did, because the mad cunt was stalking me!' Give me a break before I go mad.

One Broadmite, old Doug Hamill, was having his monthly interview with the doctor, when out of the blue he snatched the gold pen off of the doctor and swallowed it. A fucking pen. This same loon had a history of swallowing things, all sorts. A bed spring, razor blades, biros, spoons! They used to have to rush him to an outside hospital and cut him open to retrieve the items. Un-fucking-believable! The doctor actually got the pen back and had it put into a glass box, keeping it proudly on the mantelpiece in his study.

Another loon disliked his gardening job so much he stabbed himself in the foot with the garden fork. And he stabbed two more Broadmites, just for the fun of it.

Kent Block, as I said, had a pool table. One day I was sat in there when a loon walked into the day room. Without warning or any explanation, he picked up all the balls and started throwing them around the room. Some hit the loons, some smashed windows. He was soon overpowered and injected. No one knew why he did it. I doubt even he knew.

One loon, Ian Ball, was a particularly strange chap. Reportedly, on 20 March 1974, Ball held up Princess Anne's chauffeur-driven car, pointing a gun at her and her then-husband Captain Mark Phillips. He fired several times, missing them but hitting police, royal staff and a *Daily Mirror* reporter (one less reporter in the world is not a bad thing in my eyes). He was tried at the Old Bailey and remanded to Broadmoor indefinitely, where he was diagnosed as a schizophrenic. Ball claimed he was wrongly branded insane and was actually a political prisoner.

Years later, a bizarre website was launched where a supporter of Ball's claimed the whole incident was a money-making hoax. A reward of one million was offered to anyone who could prove this 'hoax'. My money's on this. He tried to kidnap Princess Anne in the 1970s because he was a fucking lunatic and it's that simple. He was one strange Broadmite, no one could work him out. He had something about royalty. He felt 'Fuck them lot. I am royalty.' He wanted to move into the palace and kick them out. Oh well, what do you expect in an asylum?

Graham Young arrived in Broadmoor in 1962 and he was just fourteen years old at the time (see Famous Inmates, page 192). He had poisoned his family so the papers imaginatively called him the 'Tea Cup Killer'. And what job do you think they gave him while he was in Broadmoor? Go on, have a guess. No? Shall I tell you? They gave him the tea boy job. I shit you not. Would you trust a poisoner to make your tea? Would I? Would I fuck!

They let him out after eight years and he poisoned his workmates. What genius members of staff made that decision? (And they called us Broadmites mad.)

You think the people in charge are the sane ones? Get on this. I've got to tell you all about this because this really illustrates what I have been saying all along about Broadmoor, that the staff were as mad as the patients, if not madder. One of the psychiatrists who certified me mad in 1978, a Dr Cooper, was himself declared insane and nutted off. Cooper was the principle medical officer at Parkhurst Prison for a good twenty years. Then he is caught one day wandering through the woods, walking his pet poodle... NAKED. Bollock naked he was caught, walking along with his crown jewels swinging like a fucking pendulum.

This proves another thing I am saying. Insanity can strike anyone and at any time. Now, I am not using this to slag the man off, because Dr Cooper was actually a decent man with a lot of kindness in his heart. It took a lot of spirit to do what he did (no, not the wandering naked through the woods). Years before, Frankie Fraser had the granny smashed out of him in the Parkhurst riots of 1960. Frank got his skull opened up by the screws' batons; he had his leg broken too and was absolutely smashed to bits. Dr Cooper stood up in a court and condemned the brutality of the screws, because he despised bullies. As you can imagine, the screws hated him after that, and he had to continue working with them. THAT takes courage, a big pair of bollocks to do that.

I always found him to be a humane man, if a little odd. He seemed to have a very feminine manner about him but he always spoke to me with conviction and truth. Don't get me wrong: we had our differences. At times he had me sedated and put in the box, or even a straitjacket. But he was still a fair man overall. Why would a man like that do something so insane as walk out naked, losing years of respectability? I reckon all those years of working with prison lunatics rubbed off on him. He took his work home and it chewed him up and spat him out.

Do you know, he came into my cell once when I was under restraint and said to me, in front of about eight watching guards, and I quote, 'You are one of the most unpredictable, dangerous prisoners we have ever had to deal with. If you continue your mission of destruction, you will find yourself in a very high secure mental institution.' Well, he was right on that front, wasn't he? Maybe we were both on a mission of madness, or did I pull him into my own dark space, maybe? He was actually a bit of a legend to me, Dr Cooper. I didn't dislike him. Why should I? If he wants to go tiptoeing through the tulips and skipping naked through the woods with the fairies, crack on. Just don't do it in my garden or you'll get my boot up your bare arse. And that isn't even the worse of it. Here's a decision that beats even The Mad Poisoner being released.

Barry Williams. Remember me telling you about him? The mad cowboy who went on a killing spree, shooting down five, in his neighbourhood? Get on this. He was released after serving fifteen years. RELEASED! Now that is what you call working the ticket. Playing the system. 'I was very poorly when I came in, but now I've found Jesus.' Where was he hiding, under your fucking mattress? 'Jesus saved me! I am no longer a danger to society. Free me.'

So multiple murdering fuckers like him get out. It sickens me. Would he kill again? Who can say? Want him as your neighbour? (Well, see page 20 for the answer.) Most of the sex cases get out, and believe me, 99 per cent of them re-offend. That is how Broadmoor works. If you're a little pet and you do as you're told and make a nice pot of tea for the guards, there's a chance for you. They let cunts like that out but they wouldn't let Ronnie Kray out. Who would you rather have living next door to you? I bet I know. I rest my case.

A load of us were in the day room one day watching a film. Everyone was settled, enjoying the flick, when a loon jumps in, runs over to the television set, grabs the wire and bites clean through it. He was electrocuting himself. Luckily a guard rushed in and switched off the mains. Now, why would anybody do that? Get me the fuck out of here… I'm a celebrity!

Broadmoor has got a lot of mice. Field mice. Obviously, being surrounded by the beautiful Berkshire countryside, it's gonna happen. And they are lovely little things, not like sewer rats or London black rats. They are gentle. Quite a few of the Broadmites had one as a pet. One old boy kept his in a shoe box, feeding it nuts and bits of bread. It was very tame. One day some fucking loon ran into the old boy's cell, grabbed his pet mouse and bit its head off. Why? Who knows. Nasty fucker. What a horrible thing to do. They never caught the culprit. You gotta laugh or you'd go insane. (I used to put black boot polish on the toilet seat. I don't know why, but why not? Relieve the boredom, I suppose, to liven the place up a bit. Remember, it's an asylum.)

I saw one fat nonce get a six-inch nail embedded in the top of his crust. No one lost sleep over the beast. It was one up for the kids he'd abused. He survived, but God will sort him out. What goes around comes around, eventually.

There was a professor of mathematics in Broadmoor. He had just flipped one day and wiped out his entire family. He just woke up and went mad. He lost everything. He was well into his sixties when he did it too, which goes to show you that it's never too late to lose your mind. Now he was counting the days, weeks and months until he hit Block 8. He'd snuffed out the ones he loved, and who loved him. Who would bury him now?! Block 8 for that crazy old fucker.

We had a totally insane fella who would go to the toilet and run out laughing hysterically, naked but for the shit he was covered in. He'd jump on one of the guards or an unfortunate loon who wasn't quick enough to get out of his way. Until you've seen such madness with your own eyes, you will never really be able to understand it. We were all shitting ourselves in case he jumped on us. It wasn't a nice sight and fuck me, the smell was worse. Dirty fucker. If he'd ever come at me I'd have chinned him. There were some filthy bastards in the asylum… and it wasn't always the loons.

Here's something that will amaze you. I actually conducted a six-month survey on the guards. My own project. You may find this interesting. I was amazed how many of them farted. Not just little ones, but massive explosions. I'm talking cheek rumblers! I was so intrigued by this I decided to keep tabs on this disgusting behaviour. I kept notes on it: culprit, age, weight, where, when, etc. And I have to say, the conclusion I drew from my findings was that they are a bunch of animals, but unique animals nonetheless. They seemed to do it: 1. For fun. 2. To try and be louder than each other. 3. To have the longest one – a good one could last for about 8–10 seconds. 4. On more than one occasion it was noted that the guard ran off to the toilet immediately after (they'd probably shit themselves). 5. The smell was disgusting. 6. They were disgusting.

I also noticed that, strangely, they NEVER farted when officials were visiting the block or when the superintendent did his daily rounds. Neither did they fart in front of visitors. Seemingly it was only us loons that they didn't mind breaking wind around, almost as though we weren't there. Filthy bastards. It means that their farts were forced, they weren't accidental – they were doing it for the sake of it. These were men in charge of our pitiful lives, and they had so little respect for us they didn't give a fuck. They'd all laugh when one of them did it. Most of them were mid-40s with great big bellies and fat arses. My survey concluded that seven out of ten of the guards on Norfolk Block were farters. The other three, to their credit, were as disgusted as us patients.

When the officials were visiting, sometimes I'd jump up and shout, 'Go on you fat slob, fart now. Why ain't you farting now, eh? Not one of you have got the bollocks to do it now.' If looks could have killed I'd be long dead.

I also made it clear to all the guards 'If you ever fart near me, I will knock you spark out!' I asked the staff that didn't do it, 'Why do you put up with it?' Surely they found it as disgusting as we did. 'Why don't you grow some bollocks and put a stop to it?' I told them. I used to keep on and on at them until they'd snap and end up shouting at their colleague about it. Ha, ha.

One would shout, 'Fucking pack it in, I'm sick of this childish behaviour!' Then I'd pipe up, 'Yeah! Have some respect for your workmates. Why should they have to put up with your disgusting behaviour?' There would then be a big argument between the two guards and me. I'd shout, 'Why should we have to sit here breathing your shit in?' Anyway, I was so relentless that in the end, it actually stopped! Get on this: they actually had a meeting about it between them, and decided to pack it in. Can you fucking believe it? Only in Broadmoor could that happen. I mean, I know people have to do it. But there's a time and a place for it: it's called the toilet. Filthy bastards. Even in prisons it happens – the screws do it, even in front of female officers. If some lazy fat bastard farted in front of my woman or mother I would give him a shock alright.

Until you've been in a day room with twenty loons all laughing, you've never lived. Believe me, there is nothing like it. But what's even more mad… we were laughing at nothing. Just laughing hysterically at nothing. It's insane but so wonderfully warming! But one old boy would sit in his chair and burst out crying. He'd sit there sobbing his heart out, and it would go on for fucking hours. I got so fed up with it one day I poured a bucket of cold water over him. I thought it would shock him into stopping. Did it fuck. It made him cry more. You just can't help some loons.

Imagine this scene if you can: I'm sitting at a dining table in a room with thirty other loons and there's three of us to a table. Now this was my very first day in the dining room. I've picked up the teapot and poured myself a cuppa. Being a sociable type of chap I thought others might like one. I started with the old loon next to me.

'Want a cuppa mate?' He just looked at me. In fact, he looked right through me. He didn't speak, he didn't nod. Nothing. What do I do? 'Oi! Cuppa mate?' He blanks me. Fuck it, I thought. I've got the teapot in my hand. I turned his cup over and poured him a cup. Then I asked the other loon at the table. 'Cuppa?' He smiled and said 'Please.' I then picked up the milk jug and poured some for myself. I turned to Mr Talkative. 'Milk?' He just looks at me. He's starting to piss me off big time. It's just fucking rude.

'MILK. DO YOU WANT MILK IN YOUR FUCKING TEA?'

I'm getting angry now. You just can't be sociable with some people. I poured some in anyway, and some in the other loon's cup. Then it happened. BANG! The old loon jumped up and started going fucking mental. He picked up the whole table and threw it up in the air. Bang goes my fucking tea! Then he picked up his chair and used it to smash the lights, and started on the windows. He had gone completely insane. But even worse, he was screaming. 'I'LL PUT MY OWN MILK IN MY OWN TEA!' It completely blew me away. I could not believe what I was seeing, and all the other loons in the room were as taken aback as me.

Guards stormed in, grabbing him and dragging him off for a very large injection. Fuck me, all because I'd put milk in his tea. What a nasty fucker I'd been, eh? I couldn't believe it (mind you, it was my first day). I made a mental note never to pour him a cuppa in future.

Oh, before I forget, I must point out – everyone else in Broadmoor called the guards 'nurse'. I called them what they were, guards. I couldn't call them nurses, they weren't. Same as the cells weren't rooms, the exercise yard was just that, not an 'airing court'. And I wasn't a patient: I was a prisoner. Broadmoor wasn't a hospital and never will be. And I'll tell you this for nothing: 99 per cent of them guards could never been seen as nurses, some of them were 20-stone freaks full of tattoos and broken noses. They were what they were, heavies. They loved a fucking rumble. What 'nurse' wears boots?

Get on this – I saved a Broadmite! I shuffled into the recess one day for a piss and walked bang into a suicide attempt. This loon had a bed sheet ripped up into strips, knotted together, and had tied it to the toilet cistern. He was just wrapping it around his neck when I walked in. I grabbed hold of him. 'Fuck me, come here son. What's your silly game?' I cared about this lad and really felt for him. I got rid of the sheet and took him for a coffee, waiting for him to unwind so he could tell me his problem.

He told me about his case. He had decapitated his mother and walked into the pig shop with her head in a carrier bag (not for the faint-hearted). I have to say this now, the lad looked as normal as you or I. He didn't look like a lunatic, or a monster, or even evil. You would never have believe he was responsible for such a horrific crime. I think he was living with the nightmare of what he had done, his mum forever looking into his eyes. It was truly a terrible thing to do.

I asked him why he did it, and he simply did not know. That was the loon's insanity. Living with it every day for the rest of his life. His own personal nightmare. It was sad really, but he was only one of many. As far as I know he never tried to top himself again (at least not in the short spell that I was on Kent Ward). But I found it so sad. The lad wanted out, straight into Block 8.

I was sitting in a chair in the day room on Kent Ward one day when a Broadmite crept up and whispered in my ear, 'I love you.' Fuck me, he must be insane. Things like that never really leave you. He loved me. What a joke. But he really meant it... and it took a lot of bottle to do that. I said to him, 'But if you loved me, *really* loved me, you'd buy me chocolates and sweets, and spoil me with gifts!' Heh heh, that was my canteen sorted. He bought me large bars of Galaxy and Cadbury's Dairy Milk, bags of toffees, all sorts. Well, I must say it's nice to be loved! You've got to laugh or you'll cry.

Speaking of which, there was a loon on Kent Block that used to piss me right off with his bawling sessions. Once he started crying it was like a fucking pantomime. He could cry for England. Buckets of tears, I am not joking, and all the theatrics that went with it. I don't know what his issue was but on one particular day he walked into the recess, sobbing again. I was having a shit in the cubicle and all I could hear was this cunt sobbing. I pulled the chain and went to the sink to wash my hands. Sob sob sob sob sob... fucking hell, I'd had enough of this. This wasn't snivelling. In fact it's not right to even call it sobbing. It was hysterical, insane wailing. I span round and kicked him straight in the bollocks. THERE! NOW you've at least got something to cry about.

No wonder I could never settle in Broadmoor. I felt surrounded by the madness, unable to sleep, relax or even switch off for a second. I needed to get some space before I actually killed one of these goons. Believe me, being thrust into the insanity of Broadmoor is not easy; it takes years to accept it and adjust to the new world you're in. I don't think I ever did accept it, actually. Why should I? I didn't deserve to be here. It is the craziest fucking institute on the planet and believe me, you have got to be mad to survive it. The madder the better in my book. Cuckoo, cuckoo, cuckoo!

I'll tell you this much, you had to watch your back on Kent Block. I was making some toast once when a big black loon came and sat right on top of the table, just watching me. Staring. No words, no smile, no acknowledgement, nothing. 'Alright mate,' I said to him. He nodded. 'Best not sit on there, because it's not for sitting on,' I said. And with that he pounced, like a fucking bed spring. He just attacked me. I picked up the nearest thing to me, a metal jug, and started hitting him over the crust with it. I smashed him half a dozen times with it. I had no choice. After an incident like that you have to be doubly alert, too. I never did find out what his problem was.

You'll love this one, this has got to be my favourite little yarn. One loon went out onto the yard one day and collected up all this freshly mown grass in a large carrier bag. He left it a few days, until it had gone brown and brittle, and then he stuffed it into little sweetie bags and sold it to all the loons on the ward as Mexican Laughing Grass. He sold twenty bags in one day! They paid him in coffee, sweets, peanut butter, fruit, all sorts of commodities.

But it soon came on top for him because the guards got involved. He was initially in trouble for drug dealing… and then it all came out it was just grass off the Broadmoor field. He got a serious warning. No harm done… and I did promise not to do it again.

I remember fondly my old pal, Geordie Freddie Mills (not to be confused with the boxer of the same name). This was Broadmite Fred, a legend. He once took his cell door clean off. You should have seen the guards run, they fucking shit themselves. Freddie chased them too, all along the ward. Fred was an awesome bloke. If you got head-butted by Fred, you stayed nutted. I first met him in Parkhurst Prison and I remember seeing him the day he attacked three guards. They couldn't control him so they nutted him off, as they did a lot of the violent prisoners in the system.

He did make it out, but sadly he ended up back in prison soon after and on many occasions. He kept in touch with me from time to time and our paths crossed again in Durham jail years later. But then, sadly, I heard he had died. However, he was a free man when he passed away, which is always nice to hear. To die a free man is a blessing for any Broadmite. Anyone who beats Block 8 is a winner. Believe it.

There is one night that will live in my memory for ever, and for all the wrong reasons, because it is the worst experience I have had in forty years locked away. Two cells up from mine was a black lad from Liverpool. He kept himself to himself and I think he had deeply embedded issues. He was very paranoid and mistrusting of everyone. He had been moved to Norfolk for attacking a guard and although he wasn't a big lad, he was very strong for his size as well as very volatile. He was a bit simple, I think, a loner type, very child-like. He couldn't read or write and I think he had learning difficulties.

What I heard this evening, I could not believe. This filthy fucking nonce of a guard was stood outside his hatch whispering to him, 'Come on, give it a pull. Let's watch. Ooh, it's a beauty. Come on, let's watch... faster. Turn on your side. That's lovely. Move your arse...' I was fucking livid, it made me feel physically sick. Beating the shit out of defenceless loons was one thing, but this was fucking sick.

I shouted out, banging on my door, 'Oi, you filthy fucking nonce! Taking advantage of the boy, you cunt! Oi!' I kept banging on my door until another guard came running along. I told him, 'Tell that cunt if I see him again I will do him good and proper. The fucking nonce!' That guard was never seen again on Norfolk Ward. I'm not suggesting he was sacked. I think it was more my threat that got him shipped out.

It is possibly the most sickening thing I'd experienced in all my time banged up, and I've seen and heard some sights, believe me. It's no secret that a lot of guards are gay, not that I give a fuck. But to do that to a Broadmite, a vulnerable boy, through his hatch... it's just sick – sick and evil. The boy wasn't even that way inclined, he probably didn't even realise what he was doing. What a sickening abuse of position.

I often wondered after that how many of the guards did that to the female loons. On nights they could do what they wanted, and believe me, they did. Listen to this. I remember one guard who really thought he was a tasty fucker. A right flash cunt he was. He thought he was God's gift to women and had the John Wayne walk to prove it. Big Elvis quiff, too. He smoked like a tart as well, blowing out smoke rings.

I remember one day one of the decent guards, a chap called Bill Peacock, had a blazing row with this flash cunt. Now Bill was a fair man, and a man's man too. You knew where you stood with him and he was one of the few who had compassion for the patients. He said to me one day, 'This is a mug's job.' He hated locking us up and he also detested some of the people he had to work with. Anyway, he had a barney with Flash Gordon and he actually kicked him in the nuts. I couldn't believe my eyes. It was beautiful. He got his right in the crackers. Sadly Bill got sacked over it. The wanker ran off and grassed him up, just like the rat he was. Every time he came within hearing distance of me I'd hiss at him like a snake. Even the other guards seemed to despise him. Sadly he wasn't a one-off rogue screw.

There was another on Gloucester Ward who used to go into patients' cells and dish out blow jobs to the Broadmites. Apparently this was going on years before I arrived and all the other guards knew about it. He just loved sucking a bell end. He spoke to me once and I remember his breath stank. Yuk, the dirty bastard. Fancy taking advantage of the loons like that. For all I knew he could have been dreaming of sucking my cock. The thought of it makes my fucking blood run cold. I never actually caught him in the act myself, but we would all see him plain as day walk into a cell for ten, fifteen minutes at a time and reappear, a big smile on his face. Sometimes he'd be in there with three loons at a time. The greedy bastard.

Without doubt the maddest Broadmite I ever met was Dennis Mercer. Dennis was the only loon I met who was so far gone that they used the drug-induced coma on him. This was a type of 'treatment' they used in the 1930s, 40s and 50s, experimenting on patients by injecting them with insulin. You know, what diabetics have to use, to stay alive? Well they used to give the loons the same thing, insulin. If you're not a diabetic your body doesn't need it, and it sends you into a coma. Don't believe me? Watch the Broadmoor documentary that came out in 2013 on Channel 5, in two parts.

Hey, did you see I was on it?! Clambering across the roof, like Spiderman. Anyway, you know I'm not making it up. It happened.

Now, Dennis was probably about eight stone, soaking wet, a slim lad, but when he blew a fuse he was awesomely strong. I am not a doctor so this diagnosis is just my humble opinion, but I would have put him down as a psychotic with a seriously paranoid personality. He was as mad as a box of frogs. They would put him to sleep for up to three days at a time, into an induced coma. It was the only way they could stop him. He used to bang his doors and the walls of his cell for days, and I do mean days. Nothing could stop him. And he used his head a lot, so he would cause himself serious injury. He'd cut his face and head to bits. It was very sad to see. He was full of lumps and bumps and didn't even seem to feel the pain he was inflicting on himself. After a session he would resemble the Elephant Man. It was very upsetting for us Broadmites to see, it was horrible to hear him crashing into the walls or door.

It had to be said, he was also very violent to others. He once attacked twelve guards in a single week. We all knew he was about to blow because he went very quiet for a few days beforehand and then BANG! It was off. This was some thirty years back now, so it's odds on Dennis is now dead, his journey of madness ending in Block 8. No man could survive decades of that. If he has any surviving family left, and they happen to be reading this, I would say to them, 'Be proud of Dennis because he was fearless and we all loved him.' So, with the greatest of respect, Dennis is my number-one-of-all-time Broadmite.

Ode to the Broadmites

We cry and we bleed
Our world is very deep
You could say dark and dreary
It's all the same when we sleep

Our doors are securely locked
Numbers for a name
We never kiss the sky
Insanity is to blame

Madmen are not so bad
Gentle souls at heart
Best you don't upset us
We will rip your life apart

Nobody understands
Our world is so unreal
A danger to the Public
How do you think we feel?

We are the Loons from Mars
You'll see us in your sleep
Some will bring an axe
In the dark you'll weep

Broadmites march together
Singing as they go
Join us if you wish
Rain or sun or snow

There was a guy in Norfolk Block who thought he was a professional poet, but he was a complete fucking idiot. He done all those lovey-dovey, silly sloppy ones. He thought he was a Romantic poet like Keats or Blake. He used to read them aloud out of the hatch of his cell in a poncey voice: 'Roses are red', and all that bollocks. I'd shout out one of mine and all the loons would cheer and bang their doors. I was the guv'nor at poetry, believe it.

CHAPTER 14

BROADMITES BOUND

(HOW TO BEST SURVIVE A NIGHT IN A STRAITJACKET)

'Until you've woken up in a straitjacket, you're not a fully, paid up member of the Loony Party!'

I first experienced a canvas jacket in 1976 in Wandsworth Prison, in the hospital wing of all places. I must confess, at the time it was quite a daunting experience, one of sheer panic. They're fucking nasty things, totally mind-blowing.

The type the prisons use are leather body belts with cuffs attached to the hips and ankle straps. These are generally only used on violent, uncontrollable prisoners. For a time I was transported around the country one of these, when I was ghosted from prison to prison. It was no big deal, they're not so bad. A little medieval maybe but you learn to live with it… especially when you ain't given a fucking choice. It's uncomfortable but it certainly keeps you on your toes. One thing you have to realise though, with any type of constraint of this nature – you have zero control; 0 per cent; you are fucked. You cannot even scratch your arse or pick your nose. You're at the mercy of the person with the key… so best not to be violent.

Now a jacket is something entirely different from a body belt. It's worse than a belt, because not only do you still have zero control, you cannot even SEE your arms or hands. You're like a fucking Mars Bar inside a wrapper, or a butterfly trying to break free of its casing. You're well and truly fucked. So… what are you gonna do? Scream? Shout? Try to kick out? How do you get through it (especially if this is your first time)? Take a piece of advice from me. All your abuse, screams and rants, they are going to keep you in that jacket even longer. Maybe a whole day, or two. OK, I'm going to tell you how best to survive and get through this (stop panicking, you'll be okay if you just listen to what I tell you).

Firstly, calm down. Deep breaths… that's it – in, out, in… and out. Slowly. Let's slow your breathing down so you're not hyperventilating yourself into a fit. What you don't want to do is have a panic or asthma attack in there, because then you truly are fucked. As you regulate your breathing, you will start to relax. Your muscles will stop contracting and the tension will start to leave your body. Can you feel yourself relaxing? Try it now. Try to tense every muscle in your body. Start with your feet and let it work upwards slowly like a creeping rigor mortis. Tense every muscle you can… and now let go of it all. Feel your body slide into a relaxed mode. Now that you're starting to relax, your stress levels will be dropping.

Now we are going to switch off mentally. Completely chill out. Close your eyes and take yourself to another place, away from this insanity, this institution. You're going to go some place in your mind where these bastards cannot restrain you, or break you. The mind is an incredibly powerful instrument and this is where you are going to use it to best effect.

You're not here; you are on a beach. Can you smell the sea air? That salty tingle mixed with the smell of the sand, the warmth of the sun hitting your head and your face. There are kids laughing as they run along the beach, a boy has a hot dog and one girl is holding an ice cream – look, she's trying to lick it quickly as it's melting and running down her hand. Can you hear the seagulls squawking? Every now and then one swoops down, picking at discarded food by a rubbish bin. As you relax on your towel you can feel the sun warming your body up, a gentle breeze every now and then. Time doesn't mean anything here. You don't have to rush back for work.

The key to this, to anything that involves using your mind, is the breathing. Get your breathing right and the body will follow. Your mind can take you anywhere you want to go, anywhere in the world – even imaginary places or places we cannot yet reach (the moon, planets!). It is only the panic and fear that causes stress. And the stress brings on the screams. So take my advice and chill out.

And here is another tip for you. Most cell walls, padded rooms, solitary pads, etc., they all have stains on the walls. They will all have something, a crack, marks. Find that something and focus on it, concentrate your mind on that one focal point and stay on it. Then watch something truly magical happen. Watch it move. Watch it grow and transform into something strangely familiar. A face, maybe a map, a piece of fruit even. But I promise you, it WILL transform itself. I've seen smiling faces come out of similar marks and stains, and if you're there long enough, with just your mind and the solitude, they may even start talking to you. Yep, you can laugh, but it's a fact.

However, you could choose to ignore my advice and spend your time doing it your way, screaming and shouting in the vain hope that someone will come and release you – all the time extending your stay in the jacket. Expect a long wait. However, it could be said that it's worth the wait. Because once you're freed, it's truly a lovely feeling. You actually appreciate life a little bit more. That's what I mean when I say loonies are a special breed. They are blessed at surviving serious shit like this in life. They survive it over and over when most would crumble like a cookie.

Broadmoor actually prefers drug-control to the belt restraint. (Oh, I must tell you this. Someone asked me recently, 'If Broadmoor patients are 'Broadmites', what are Rampton patients called? And what about Ashworth Hospital?' Well I'd say Ramptonites… Ashworth? Who the fuck knows? I've been in all three, but that's another story, for another day. This is Broadmoor we're talking about.) Need something to remind you? Let me tell you about the Broadmite who caused the entire asylum to be redecorated one day. The WHOLE fucking asylum. That truly is going some, isn't it? Want to know how he achieved it? Here's how…

He was in a seclusion cell one day and he decided to cut himself. He was naked and the cell was completely empty, yet he managed to cut himself so badly he very nearly bled to death. 'But Charlie,' I hear you ask, 'how did he do that? What did he use to cut himself with, in seclusion, in a mental hospital?' You may well ask. Paint flakes. Consider this: Over the course of decades, the walls had had about twenty to thirty paints of coat. He began to pick away at the wall until he had peeled off big enough strips of paint, and he then proceeded to cut himself up. He sliced into his wrists, groin and neck. Blood pissed out all over the place.

Subsequently, they had to strip down the walls to the brickwork, and repaint the WHOLE asylum with a special spray paint that didn't flake. Now THAT'S insanity. In more than a hundred years of existence the place ticks along and then a mad incident like that can cause a complete policy change.

That's why loonies are so special, you see. They see things the sane person would never see, and when they choose to call it a day they can and will find a way. One loon achieved it by running straight into a wall, breaking his neck. Some, I'm saddened to say, want a place in Block 8 way before their allotted time. Broadmoor has been through quite a few stages of redevelopment and had new blocks added, and others pulled down, but I wonder what happened to Block 8. Has it been built over, or is it still there? Imagine if they dug it up to rebuild on it. I bet there's a few eerie, ghostly goings-on, don't you? I fucking hope so. We do love a naughty Broadmite spirit!

I'm not really sure about the meaning of life any more. All I really know is how best to survive. No one on this planet knows that better than me. Broadmites have a special way of dealing with certain issues. We have a switch that we can flick on in times of stress. It cuts us off from reality and puts us in the world of insanity. Without that switch it's Block 8. It's really that simple.

I guess no one knows the real end. Let's face it – it wouldn't be nice to know, would it? Maybe our end is only the beginning… Who even cares? Fuck me, I'm getting all philosophical again. LIFE is all that matters. A sparkle of hope. That beautiful rainbow. A dream. A desire. Whatever it is that makes you want to wake up to another day. If you're not like this, you're already defeated. Lost within, with no way back perhaps. You kill your own dreams. I watched many in Broadmoor do that. They simply gave up: it squeezed all of the life out of them. The tube is empty (granted for some the tube was half empty to start with!). But I think Broadmites are actually very lucky people. Simply because they are living a part of history inside the most famous mental institution in the world. Come on, it don't get any better than that.

Okay, I've given you the guided tour as it were. You've been through five years of hell with me. Hey, we're both still here; that has to count for something. I hope it's given you a better understanding of Hellmoor, and how it made me the person I am today. How did I survive it? Who the fuck knows? I'll leave you with these last few words, my parting thoughts on Broadmoor.

EPILOGUE

'I reached the end of the rainbow, and there wasn't a pot of gold…
just a fucking car park!'

I couldn't have done my time any other way than how I did it. If I had, I would have died a broken man. My whole being and purpose to life was, and always will be, to enjoy it. Even the bad times are good for me. Sure, sometimes it was a bit naughty and dangerous and unpredictable. But even free people jump in front of trains or off of bridges, or blow their heads off. There is a great sense of worth buried in a lifetime of insanity, memories I have of achieving impossible things. They are always there in my brain and no one can take them away from me.

I don't hate Broadmoor. I actually feel sorry for the bully boys and the evil doctors because their memories must be shameful ones, that chew them up if and when they are forced to remember them. A coward's memory must be the worst sort to live with. When they reach old age and they know they are close to death, it's them that will be their own victims. I feel great warmth for all the Broadmites.

(Well, all but the evil slags whose crimes of insanity were against children. I hope Block 8 sucks them under while they are still breathing. Buried alive.)

And please, let's not forget Michael Martin. He was just one of so many who died unjustly and avoidably, a victim of the system and the people who turned its handle. Maybe it's time for some of those involved in his death and other heinous crimes that took place behind those walls to come forward, to speak the truth and seek penance. At least you'll be able to go on and die a happy soul and not a tormented one. I might have been called a nut and a lunatic and 'Britain's most violent prisoner', but I couldn't live with being a coward. I would sooner walk to Block 8, slit my throat and call it a day.

However, I made it out of the hellhole, so I know I am one of the lucky ones. I could have easily instead been one of the forgotten ones. Not that I am saying my journey has been a happy one. Because it's now forty-one years, and I am still locked up. For all but three months of freedom I have been caged up in max secure jails. As I write this I am in Woodhill, the close-supervision centre (CSC) designed for murderers and exceptional risk prisoners. Fuck-all has changed in the eyes of the system: I am and always will be an ex-Broadmoor lunatic. It never leaves you.

I have only one regret from my time there: why the fuck didn't I pull that roof off the third time when I had the opportunity to? I was a mug to believe the bollocks they fed me. Then again, who knows, maybe I would have died up there that day… and then you would never have read this story. This is my testament to the atrocities that happened in that hellhole.

Today I am a prolific artist, an acclaimed writer with some sixteen books to my name, an award-winning poet, a singer, a ventriloquist (it's true), a Scrabble King… oh, and I dance. My art has been shown around the world in various forms. In November 2012, I passed a Violence Reduction Programme that NO ONE in the history of the CSC has done. I am also engaged to a beautiful lady, a real cockney sparra.

I am living proof that there is life after Life. Sure it's bloody hard to live your past down and shake off your skeletons, the insanity never really leaves you. You just learn to keep it under control. With age and maturity and by applying a bit of common sense, you keep it under control. You have to find other ways of expressing your emotions and frustrations. The biggest thing for me was my art. Art saved me, along with my lady's love. Oh, and she is a Lorraine. So now I have two of them in my life, Loraine and Lorraine. Two angels. So I am double blessed! You could say this Broadmite done good. I'm still not there yet, though. My goal is to walk free and get on with what's left of my journey, in freedom. I'll leave you with this last fact:

UP YOURS BLOCK 8 – HERE'S ONE LUNATIC YOU NEVER GOT!

'I kissed the rainbow, the rainbow kissed me, now my life's so colourful, it's time to set me free.'

POSTSCRIPT – OCTOBER 2014

Well, I bet you're all wondering what's happened to old Charlie boy since I left the asylums. Well, let me tell ya. Fuck-all changes. I'm still suffering the same shit now that I was back then.

Since moving from Monster Mansion (Wakefield Prison) to Woodhill, things didn't go good. Within a week my post was being messed about with. Then the same old games started. My art was stopped from going out. Even a Valentine's piece I did for my Lorraine was stopped. I wasn't even notified. They just held on to my mail for weeks on end, when I thought it had been posted out. It was a diabolical liberty. A blow-up was on the cards and they knew it. Some say they planned it that way. Who knows? Anyway, I got two years added to my sentence. TWO YEARS, for a slap! I am now back on the HMP merry-go-round, where they just move me from block to block, prison to prison, at short notice and without warning. Who gives a fuck? I've have over forty years of it now. You won't hear me crying like the cons of today. 'I've lost my Playstation. My TV's gone.' Do me a favour.

Anyway, a new era beckons! 1 September 2014 was an historical day – the day Bronson died and Salvador was born. That's right. He is buried. History. Bronson created fear and chaos wherever he went, with cons and screws alike. Well, no more. Salvador is an artist, a peace-loving creator. My art has been my saviour and I will continue to create, under my new name and identity. Anyone who don't understand or don't like it can get the fuck off the train now, 'cos I ain't got time for hangers-on and wannabe gangsters. I am an artist. I despise violence and crime. I was never a good criminal. But I'm a bloody good artist. My art is unique, it has been shown around the world. Salvador is going to be my saviour.

Now don't think I'm going soft in my old age. I can still dish out a slap if people take liberties with me. But I don't want or need it any more. I've nothing to prove, to myself or others. I am going to set the art world alight.

Remember, keep punching till the lights go out!

Your old china,

Charlie.

[For more information on Charlie and his art, please visit: http:// charlessalvador.com]

APPENDIX I

BROADMOOR: FAMOUS INMATES

Broadmoor has housed some of the most notorious, prolific and violently dangerous people the country has seen. The mad and the bad have all spent time at Broadmoor, and this role call of dishonour gives you a brief insight into a selection of the infamous characters that have become legendary Broadmites.

RICHARD DADD (1 AUGUST 1817–7 JANUARY 1886)

Dadd was born in Kent, England, and showed an early talent for art, leading to his admission to the Royal Academy of Arts at the age of twenty. He was awarded the medal for life drawing in 1840. Towards the end of December 1842, while travelling up the Nile, Dadd underwent a dramatic personality change, becoming delusional and increasingly violent. On his return to England in 1843, he was diagnosed to be of unsound mind and was taken to recuperate in the countryside of Cobham, Kent.

By August of that year, he became convinced that his father was the Devil and killed him with a knife, before fleeing for France. En route, Dadd attempted to kill another tourist with a razor, but was overpowered and arrested by the police. He confessed to the killing of his father and was returned to England, committed to Bethlem mental institution (also known as Bedlam).

In July 1864 he was transferred to newly created Broadmoor, where he was allowed to continue to paint. From here, he created many of his masterpieces including his most famous work *The Fairy Feller's Master-Stroke*, which he worked on between 1855 and 1864. His work was executed with a miniaturist's eye for detail, which belied the fact they were products of imagination and memory. Dadd remained in Broadmoor until 17 January 1886, when he died of lung disease.

KENNETH ERSKINE (BORN JULY 1962 OR JULY 1963 – SOURCES DIFFER)

Nicknamed the 'Stockwell Strangler', Erskine murdered at least seven elderly people in 1986 alone, breaking into their homes and strangling them; often they were also sexually assaulted.

It was clear to the police that all these attacks were the work of one man. In all cases, there were no signs of forced entry, with every indication that the intruder had gained access through an unsecured window. In each case it appeared that the killer had knelt on the victim's chest, then placed his left hand over their mouth while using his right to grip their throat and strangle them to death. In addition, four of the victims had been sodomised, although there was some uncertainty as to whether this had taken place before or after death.

Erskine was arrested on 28 July 1986 at a social security office and police were then able to match his palm print to one left at one of the murder scenes. He was also identified in a police line-up by a 74-year-old man who claimed Erskine had tried to strangle him in his bed a month before police had apprehended him.

A homeless drifter and solvent abuser, Erskine committed his heinous crimes when he was twenty-two to twenty-three years old. He was convicted of the seven known murders, although police suspected him of a further four. During his trial, he was witnessed to be masturbating. Erskine was sentenced to life imprisonment with a recommended minimum term of forty years, but was later diagnosed with a mental disorder and sectioned to Broadmoor, believed to be suffering chronic schizophrenia and antisocial personality disorder.

In July 2009, following an appeal, Erskine's murder convictions were reduced to manslaughter on the grounds of diminished responsibility. Erskine was scolded by the court for falling asleep during the proceedings and, at one point, snoring. Some twenty-eight years later, the trial judge's recommendation is still one of the most severe ever handed out in British legal history.

RON KRAY (24 OCTOBER 1933–17 MARCH 1995)

One half of the infamous Kray Twins, Ronald Kray was born in the tough East End of London, in Bethnal Green, and along with brother Reginald, was predominantly raised by their mother Violet Lee. Along with elder brother Charlie, the Krays took up amateur boxing, and their success extended beyond the ring, with the twins developing a reputation for troublemaking and narrowly escaping criminal conviction on a number of occasions.

In March 1952, both twins were called for national service. Frequent desertion resulted in a spell in military prison before they were handed a dishonourable discharge. Subsequent criminal records meant their hopes of a professional boxing career were scuppered.

Ron and Reg built a criminal empire that was reportedly run on fear, developing operations that included racketeering, hijacking, armed robbery and arson. Police were aware of their activities, but their merciless reputations made it impossible for police forces to persuade witnesses to bring evidence against the twins.

On 9 March 1966, in what was believed to be a dispute between the Krays and the Richardson gang, Ron entered the Blind Beggar public house in Whitechapel, East London and shot Richardson's' associate George Cornell in the head. He was killed instantly. On 8 May 1968 the police, believing they had enough evidence, arrested the Kray brothers Ron and Reg, along with fifteen members of their 'firm'. Many witnesses came forward and both Ron and Reg and fourteen others were convicted, with one member of the firm being acquitted.

By 1979, Ron had been diagnosed as a paranoid schizophrenic and transferred from the prison system to Broadmoor. Ronald Kray died of a heart attack in Broadmoor Hospital on 17 March 1995.

ROBERT MAUDSLEY (BORN 26 JUNE 1953)

Maudsley was one of twelve children born in Toxteth, Liverpool, and he spent most of his early years in an orphanage run by nuns. At the age of eight, he was retrieved by his parents and beaten regularly until he was eventually removed from their care by social services.

During the late 1960s, the teenage Maudsley became a rent boy in London to support his drug addiction. He was finally forced to seek psychiatric help after several suicide attempts. He claimed to hear voices telling him to kill his parents and reported that he was raped as a child. In 1973, Maudsley garrotted a man who picked him up for sex after the man showed Maudsley pictures of children he had sexually abused. He was sentenced to life imprisonment with a recommendation that he should never be released, and sent to Broadmoor.

In 1977, Maudsley and fellow patient John Cheeseman took a convicted child molester hostage and locked themselves in a cell, torturing him to death over a period of nine hours. Maudsley was convicted of manslaughter and sent to Wakefield Prison. In 1978 he killed two more fellow prisoners, Salney Darwood and Bill Roberts. He hacked at Roberts' skull with a makeshift dagger and smashed his head against the wall.

In 1983, Maudsley was deemed too dangerous for a normal cell and placed in the close supervision centre at Wakefield, Yorkshire. He remains in a cell twenty-three hours a day.

DR WILLIAM CHESTER MINOR (JUNE 1834–26 MARCH 1920)

American army surgeon W C Minor passed through the forbidding gates of Broadmoor Criminal Lunatic Asylum in April 1872, to begin an incarceration that lasted thirty-eight years.

Engaged in the American Civil War, he had been strongly drawn to the red light area of the city and spent increasing amounts of time and money on prostitutes. His behaviour became increasingly bizarre and by 1868, Minor showed growing signs of mental instability and was placed in St. Elizabeth's Hospital, the US government hospital for the insane.

In 1871 Minor he was discharged from the hospital and came to London. Here he resumed his liaisons with prostitutes and, his paranoia returning, carried a loaded gun. Early on 17 February 1872, Minor woke up believing someone was trying to get into his room. He chased after and shot at a man in the street: George Merrett, a 34-year-old stoker at the Lion Brewery was killed. Minor was judged not guilty on grounds of insanity and detained as a 'certified criminal lunatic' at Broadmoor.

Minor was allocated two rooms in the 'swells block' at Broadmoor and was allowed books and painting materials. He is most notable as becoming a contributor of quotations to the first edition of the *Oxford English Dictionary*, but by 1902 his mental health had deteriorated and he cut off his penis in an act of self-mutilation, an act he thought would stop his lascivious thoughts.

In 1910, following strong representations from Dr Murray, of the *Oxford English Dictionary* and the US Consulate, the then Home Secretary, Winston Churchill, signed the necessary papers to allow Minor to return to his former mental hospital in the USA. He died of complications arising from pneumonia on 26 March 1920 in an old people's home in New Haven. The last psychiatric diagnosis on Minor was that he was suffering from dementia praecox, or schizophrenia.

ALAN REEVE (BORN 1949)

Reeve was sent to Broadmoor in 1964 after killing a friend when they were both only fifteen. While in Broadmoor he got a sociology degree – and strangled fellow patient, Billy Doyle.

In 1981 he escaped with the help of his girlfriend. Reeve was on the run for a year, before being arrested in the Netherlands in 1982 following a gunfight at a liquor store during which he killed chief constable, Jaap Honingh. He was sentenced to fifteen years in prison for this crime. In 1992, he was released on parole but the Dutch courts refused to extradite him back to Britain.

He lived for the next five years in Ireland. Before his arrest in 1997, he managed to obtain a law degree in the Netherlands, father a son and work as a typesetter for Cork Women's Poetry Circle. He spent another five months in Broadmoor before it was finally declared that he was no longer a threat to society and he was released.

APPENDIX I

JOHN STRAFFEN (27 FEBRUARY 1930–19 NOVEMBER 2007)

Serial killer Straffen was, at the time of his death, the longest-serving prisoner in British legal history, serving fifty-five years. In July 1951, Straffen kidnapped and strangled six-year-old Brenda Goddard. A few days later, he befriended a nine-year-old girl called Cecily Batstone at a local cinema and subsequently strangled her. When he was arrested he immediately confessed to the two murders and was sent to trial, where he was found unfit to plead and committed to Broadmoor Hospital.

During a brief escape from Broadmoor on 29 April 1952, he was free for only a few hours when he came across five-year-old Linda Bowyer on her bike. He strangled the little girl to death. Interviewed the following day, he stated that he had 'not killed the little girl on her bike', before the police had even mentioned a missing child. Straffen was convicted of murder and sentenced to death. Reprieved because of his mental state, he had his sentence commuted to life imprisonment and he remained in various prisons until his death, at the age of seventy-seven.

PETER SUTCLIFFE (BORN 2 JUNE 1946)

Nicknamed 'The Yorkshire Ripper', Sutcliffe terrorised the area of Yorkshire in a five-year reign of terror, attacking prostitutes and killing thirteen women. The cases were connected by his consistent method of murder, first striking his victim with a hammer and then stabbing and mutilating them.

In 1969, Sutcliffe committed his first known violent crime. While out with a friend, he attacked a prostitute with a stone stuffed in a sock, striking her on the head with it. The victim escaped when the sock broke and the stone fell out. He was arrested again in October when he was caught hiding behind a lawn in Bradford carrying a hammer and a knife. He was charged with being 'equipped for theft' and fined £25.

In 1977 Sutcliffe killed Jayne MacDonald, a sixteen-year-old schoolgirl. The media labelled her as the first of his 'innocent' victims; it later emerged that he had in fact committed four other murders before then, as well as several attempted murders that the victims somehow survived.

Sutcliffe himself was interviewed a total of nine times by police over the course of the investigation, but his luck with evading the law continued. Finally, on 2 January 1981, he was caught driving a car with false licence plates with a prostitute in the car. Pretending to leave to urinate, he hid his murder weapons before being arrested. They were found the next day when police returned to the scene.

Finally, on 4 January, Sutcliffe confessed to being the Yorkshire Ripper, confessing his many assaults and murders. In court, he tried to claim diminished capacity, saying he had heard voices from God telling him to kill prostitutes. Though diagnosed with paranoid schizophrenia, the judge rejected the claim and Sutcliffe was found guilty of thirteen murders and sentenced to a minimum of thirty years in prison.

He was later diagnosed with schizophrenia and sent to Broadmoor in 1984. Several attempts have been made on his life, once of which resulted in him losing the sight in one eye. In 2010, his sentence was extended to a full life term and he is still there.

GRAHAM YOUNG (10 SEPTEMBER 1947–1 AUGUST 1990)

Born in Neasden, north London, Graham Young was a serial killer who used poison to kill his victims. He became interested in chemistry, forensic science and toxicology from an early age and was particularly fascinated by poisons.

Young's first victim was pupil Christopher Williams, who suffered vomiting, cramps and headaches due to a cocktail of poisons that left doctors baffled. Williams was lucky to survive. Realising he couldn't fully monitor his experimentation when the victim was sick at home, Young decided to focus on those closer to home, his family.

After poisoning several members of his family and making them violently ill, and then killing his stepmother, Young was arrested and confessed; he was sent to Broadmoor in 1962. Aged only fourteen, he was the youngest patient to enter Broadmoor since the Victorian era.

Deemed 'fully recovered', he was released with fatal consequences in 1971, as he went on to poison seventy more people at his place of work, two of whom died. Young, who was known as the 'Teacup Poisoner', was then sent to Parkhurst Prison where he died of natural causes in 1990.

APPENDIX II

DRUGS INDEX

1. CHLORAL HYDRATE

Once used as a sedative and hypnotic drug, chloral hydrate is used for the short-term treatment of insomnia and as a sedative. Chloral hydrate has not been approved for use in the United States or the European Union for any medical indication and is on the list of unapproved drugs that is still prescribed by some clinicians. 'Usage of the drug as a sedative or hypnotic may carry some risk, given the lack of clinical trials.' [Wikipedia: http://en.wikipedia.org/wiki/Chloral_hydrate, 27 October 2013]

Side effects include nausea and/or vomiting, stomach pains, dizziness, drowsiness, clumsiness and diarrhoea.

2. LARGACTIL (CHLORPROMAZINE)

Used to treat serious mental and emotional disorders such as severe depression or behavioural disturbances. Largactil is also administered for cases of schizophrenia and other psychotic disorders. It is colloquially known as 'the liquid cosh' among patients and prisoners for its ability to knock out patients, like a cosh over the head. Known side effects are drowsiness, abnormal body movements (twitching), anxiety, restlessness, dry mouth, insomnia, nightmares and weight gain.

3. MODECATE (*FLUPHENAZINE*)

Used for the treatment of psychosis such as schizophrenia, bipolar disorder, dementia and agitation. Side effects can include raised blood pressure, drowsiness, weight gain, erectile dysfunction, dry mouth, constipation, blurred vision, tremors, restlessness, muscle rigidity, dizziness, agitation, anxiety, depression and headaches among other symptoms. Potentially irreversible side effects include tardive dyskinesia (involuntary, repetitive body movements) and the potentially fatal neuroleptic malignant syndrome (muscle rigidity, fever, and autonomic instability).

4. STELAZINE (*TRIFLUOPERAZINE*)

Primarily used for schizophrenia, Stelazine is also administered for severe anxiety and patients with behavioural problems. Side effects include dry mouth, tremors, restlessness and uncontrolled muscle contractions causing abnormal postures.

5. TARACTAN (CHLORPROTHIXENE, CLOXAN, TRUXAL)

An anti-psychotic drug* used in cases of psychotic disorders such as schizophrenia and acute mania occurring as part of bipolar disorder. Taractan has strong sedative potency with side effects such as dry mouth, high blood pressure, tachycardia (irregular heart beat), and substantial weight gain. Administered in the form of a thick red syrup, Taractan is a form of tranquilliser.

---

*In his book *Inside Ashworth*, David Pilgrim states that terms like 'anti-psychotics' are misleading. He counters, 'some people benefit some of the time from pharmacological solutions. Others remain unaffected or may fluctuate in their functioning, whether or not they are treated.' (Pilgrim, page 14)

APPENDIX III

OFFICIAL CHANGE OF NAME

Official Statement of Charles Bronson, No 1314, Cat A

Date: 28/07/14

Full Sutton Prison, York YO4 1PS

I have given this a lot of thought and I really have little choice but to kill Bronson off once and for all. I have become a hostage of my own notoriety, Bronson is burying any chance of me ever being freed.

It was back in 1987 that the Bronson name came about over my prize fighting era and its been with me ever since. 27 years I have lived under Bronson and all its done is cause me massive problems; violence, madness and lots of insane years.

My birth name was Michael Peterson which later became Mad Mickey Peterson, who caused havoc to the prison system. He became one of Britain's most feared inmates, he ended up being certified criminally insane and locked up in the asylums. Again he is buried, I don't wish to bring him back not until I am freed.

So I've decided to change my name by deed poll to Charles Arthur Salvador.

My reasons for this are simple! (I need some peace) It's my way of escaping myself. It's a way of starting afresh plus I am a serious artist. I'm actually a big fan of the great Salvador Dali so through my art, maybe a little part of Dali lives on in respect not that in anyway do I see myself as the great man (my art is totally different), Dali was after all a genius.

In fact the late Lord Longford once wrote in a book I am a genius, fuck knows why he claimed that but I can certainly live with that.

Bronson has really gone too far, wherever he goes follows fear. He only has to land in a prison and it spreads so many problems; screws are on the edge, Governors are alerted, prisoners expect trouble, some want to fight me, some even dream of killing me whilst others fear me. Bronson is now a target wherever I go, I can't escape it. It's actually become a complete joke after all I am a 62 year old man living in a bloody nightmare inside a concrete coffin.

I'm like the great Jesse James, everybody wanted to shoot him to get a reputation and they did. He got it in the back like most legends end up, a big hole in the back. Salvador is about

Signed: Dated:

to come alive, a peaceful chap, a man of creativity, as man of pride, a talent with a magical gift of life.

My art has already smashed its way into the art world, but that was the Bronson art. This is now the Salvador art; more intense, more detailed, more explosive, deeper and darker. I'm about to create something very special, it feels right, it's come at a good time, a great time in my life (unplanned) it just came to me like in a dream: Slow down Charlie boy! Focus! You don't need all this pressure and stress of never knowing where the next act of violence comes from. You need a rest from it all (so does the penal system) so does your family and friends. I feel like I've been at war for 4 decade, 40 years of prison and asylum life has finally sunk into my soul…"change now – or die inside".

I need to concentrate more on myself, my own issues, sort out my own problems. Rather than be on alert all the time, on my guard, I'm like a coiled spring, never ever easy or relaxed. Now Salvador is here to change it all. I predict in a years' time, Bronson will be forgotten and I'll be just like any normal prisoner, going about what we do best to get through our time peacefully.

I'm weeks away from a Bronson trial and I aim to come out of this trial Salvador, so I will win even if I lose…and I start my new journey as a brand new character, a very happy soul, free of violence and destruction, a born again artist.

If people can't see this as a positive move or a change for a better future then all I can say is 'get the fuck out of my life now' because Bronson is no longer around.

Once I'm free, sure there will be the odd Bronson prize fight or show, a guy's gotta eat and buy his old duchess a fur coat, but art is now the real me, I live for it; Salvador is born!

It should be a massive relief to all prison Governors and Home Office officials that I've taken this action. I hope you will all support my decision and make sure to assist me in my progression through your prison system. Let's have a nice, gentle, peaceful journey. A nice gesture would be to allow me out of isolation and stick me up on a normal wing so my fellow convicts can see my transformation. Maybe I could even be allowed to start up an art class…the worlds an oyster.

Onwards and Upwards (no going back).

Signed: Dated:

UK Deed Poll Service

Certified copy of a Deed of Change of Name (Deed Poll)

BY THIS DEED OF CHANGE OF NAME made by myself the undersigned Charles Arthur SALVADOR of Her Majesty's Prison, Full Sutton, York, YO41 1PS and 68 Western Drive, Hanslope, Milton Keynes, Buckinghamshire, MK19 7LE formerly known as Michael Gordon PETERSON and also known as Charles BRONSON

HEREBY DECLARE AS FOLLOWS:

1. I ABSOLUTELY and entirely renounce, relinquish and abandon the use of my former names of Michael Gordon PETERSON and Charles BRONSON and assume, adopt and determine to take and use from the date hereof the name of Charles Arthur SALVADOR in substitution for my former names of Michael Gordon PETERSON and Charles BRONSON

2. I SHALL at all times hereafter in all records, deeds, documents and other writings and in all actions and proceedings, as well as in all dealings and transactions and on all occasions whatsoever use and subscribe the said name of Charles Arthur SALVADOR as my name, in substitution for my former names of Michael Gordon PETERSON and Charles BRONSON so relinquished as aforesaid to the intent that I may hereafter be called, known or distinguished by the name of Charles Arthur SALVADOR only

3. I AUTHORISE and require all persons at all times to designate, describe and address me by the adopted name of Charles Arthur SALVADOR

IN WITNESS whereof I have hereunto subscribed my adopted and substituted forenames of Charles Arthur and my adopted and substituted surname of SALVADOR and also my said former name of Michael Gordon PETERSON

Dated this 22nd day of AUGUST in the year 2014

SIGNED AS A DEED AND DELIVERED
by the above named
Charles Arthur SALVADOR

Signed as Charles Arthur SALVADOR

Formerly known as
Michael Gordon PETERSON
and also known as Charles BRONSON

Signed as Michael Gordon PETERSON

In the presence of:

Name ROBERT ASHMAN

Witness's signature

Address CRIMINAL DEFENCE SOLICITORS

237/239 STRAND

LONDON WC2R 1GF

Occupation LEGAL REPRESENTATIVE

We hereby certify this to be a true copy
of the original Deed Poll issued by us.

MICHAEL BARRATT, B.Sc. (Hons)
Chief Executive Officer, UK Deed Poll Service
Telephone: +44 (0)333 444 8484
E-mail: enquiries@deedpoll.org.uk

This is a colour photocopy of an original Deed Poll document issued by us, which we have certified to be a true copy of the original. Please note, this document is a genuine certified copy if it is printed on UK Deed Poll Service watermarked paper. If you are in any doubt as to this document's authenticity, please call us.

Charlie's official deed-poll certificate recording
his change of name, August 2014.

BIBLIOGRAPHY

Bronson, Charles, *Insanity: My Mad Life* (John Blake, London, 2003)

Bronson, Charles, *Legends, Volume 1* (Mirage, Gateshead, 2000)

Bronson, Charles, *Silent Scream* (Mirage, Gateshead, 1999)

Goldstein, Ezra, *John, Reid our lips: a change has got to come* (http://www.blaqfair.com/blaqfair/dthcustody/rocky.htm)

Nash, Jay Robert, *World Encyclopaedia of 20th Century Murder* (Headline, London, 1992)

Ndegwa, David and Olajide, Dele, *Main Issues in Mental Health and Race*, Volume 13 (Ashgate, Hants, 2013)

Pilgrim, David, *Inside Ashworth: Professional Reflections of Institutional Life* (Radcliffe, London, 2007)

Ritchie, Shirley, *Report to the Secretary of State for Social Services Concerning the Death of Mr Michael Martin at Broadmoor Hospital on 6th July 1984* (Dept. of Health & Social Security, 1986)

Of online resources, a short list is given below, but not included are excellent articles on Wikipedia (www.en.wikipedia.org/) about notable inmates of Broadmoor, as well as articles on individual drugs, which are easily accessed by anyone seeking more information.

www.bbc.co.uk/legacies/myths_legends/england/berkshire/article_1. shtml (accessed 31 December 2013)

www.blaqfair.com/blaqfair/dthcustody/rocky-prn.htm (accessed 23 November 2013)

www.crimeandinvestigation.co.uk/crime-files/graham-young/ biography.html (accessed 28 December 2013)

www.criminalminds.wikia.com/wiki/Peter_Sutcliffe (Accessed 28 December 2013)

www.hansard.millbanksystems.com/written_answers/1992/dec/10/ dr-kypros-loucas#S6CV0215PO_19921210_CWA 308 (accessed 18 September 2013)

www.en.wikipedia.org/wiki/Alan_Reeve (accessed 28 December 2013)

www.en.wikipedia.org/wiki/Broadmoor_Hospital (accessed 28 December 2013)

www.wlmht.nhs.uk/bm/broadmoor-hospital (accessed 28 December 2013)